Alone at the Top

Map of Denali showing the West Buttress route with main camps. *Photo courtesy of the National Park Service*

Alone at the Top

Climbing Denali in the Dead of Winter

Lonnie Dupre
with
Pam Louwagie

MINNESOTA
HISTORICAL
SOCIETY PRESS

This narrative is derived from the best of Lonnie Dupre's memory,
with sections enhanced from his notes and recordings. Quotations from his
journals, both written and audio, have been lightly edited for readability.

www.mnhspress.org

The Minnesota Historical Society Press is a member of the
Association of University Presses.

Manufactured in the United States of America

10 9 8 7 6 5 4 3 2 1

♾ The paper used in this publication meets the minimum
requirements of the American National Standard for Information Sciences—
Permanence for Printed Library Materials, ANSI Z39.48–1984.

International Standard Book Number
ISBN: 978-1-68134-082-1 (paperback)
ISBN: 978-1-68134-083-8 (e-book)

Library of Congress Cataloging-in-Publication Data
available upon request.

This and other Minnesota Historical Society Press books are
available from popular e-book vendors.

Contents

Chapter 1   An Omission / 1

2   The Fledgling Explorer / 5

3   Cold Love / 15

4   Denali Calls / 24

5   Mount Denial / 31

6   Thinking of Going Alone / 47

7   Making It Happen / 53

8   Try, Try Again / 60

9   One More Try / 74

10   Weaving through the Kahiltna
(6,700 FEET TO 9,400 FEET) / 84

11   Storm Brewing
(9,400 TO 11,200 FEET) / 92

12   Stuck / 97

13   Still Stuck / 102

Chapter 14 Atrophy in the Tent / 107

15 End Is Near / 110

16 Happy New Year! / 116

17 Forging Ahead
(CARRYING A CACHE TO 12,300 FEET) / 122

18 Getting around Windy Corner
(13,500 TO 14,200 FEET) / 125

19 Waiting to Commit
(16,200 TO 16,300 FEET) / 129

20 Go for It / 137

21 Seizing Summit Day / 143

22 Long Way Home / 150

Epilogue / 159

Acknowledgments / 165

APPENDIX A Divvying Up Weights:
A Method for Fair Distribution of Expedition
Supplies across a Team, by Pascale Marceau and
Lonnie Dupre / 171

APPENDIX B How to Keep Feet Warm
at −60°F / 176

APPENDIX C Clothing, Equipment, and
Food List / 178

APPENDIX D Live Simply to Live / 187

About the Authors / 189

Denali
Winter
Solo

Thought about it
     a year

Sometimes it seems right
Sometimes not . . .

But mountains have been my steady
     friends

Sources of inspiration
Mirror of my soul
Once again I look there for
answers.

I committed myself to the idea.

This time it will be solo . . .

This would be a test of just me.

It will be good to return to this
Starkly beautiful world of
     deep blues
     brilliant whites
     thin air
where security lies in houses of snow.

In the hills I like myself. . . . I
     reestablish some confidence, at
     least in winter mountaineering,

and I don't at all get bush
crazy in isolation. . . .
        (no crazier than usual)

Quite the opposite
        I come alive. . . .

It's by getting away from life that
we can see it most clearly. . . .
It's by depriving ourselves of the
myriad of everyday experiences
that we renew our appreciation for them:
        People's smiles, water running,
        children, warm rooms, trees,
        unfrozen boots and socks, my dogs,
        indoor toilets.

        I've learned from my experiences (in
        the mountains) that I love life.

This eloquent quotation is from Dave Johnston, a team member of the first winter ascent of Denali in 1967. He later tried to climb the mountain solo in February 1986. It clearly states my feelings about soloing Denali in winter.

Dave concludes with this quotation:

Nature nurtures the body in sight and air, but be sweet and rest the body every now and then.

Chapter 1

An Omission

Maybe it was the slow rhythm that lulled me.

Shuffle, shuffle, exhale.

I was on my ninth day of skiing *up* the mountain, most of it plowing through powdery snow so deep that I sank in past my knees with each glide. The straps of my backpack dug into my shoulders, cutting through layers of down and polyester. Tethered to my torso, an unruly sled full of heavy gear kept trying to yank me down. At my side, I dragged a thirteen-foot, three-inch-diameter black spruce tree trunk, my insurance plan for halting a crevasse fall.

I was back on Denali, completely alone, for the fourth time, on a quest to reach the highest peak in North America in the darkest, coldest, bleakest span of winter without any help. Each time before, unpredictable mountain blizzards had knocked me back, forcing me to retreat to base camp and wait for a plane to whisk me back to safety. I wasn't foolish enough to think that I could conquer nature. But often, I had found, the biggest challenges were getting through sheer exhaustion and enduring the mind-numbing mundane.

Focus! I told myself in a constant battle to keep my attention on my movements, my spirit just as tired as my fifty-three-year-old body. *Think about where the crevasses might be hiding under all this white.* If I let my mind wander to thoughts of my family and friends back home in Minnesota—gathered around cozy fireplaces; eating fresh, warm food; and engrossed in conversation—I could lose my concentration up here . . . and lose my life.

But the truth was home wasn't the same anymore. I'd started this solo climbing quest not long after my twenty-year marriage ended, and I found myself suddenly feeling completely alone. Divorce forces you to take stock of your life like nothing else, and on this mountain quest, I was figuring out my new identity. Immersed alone in such a magnificent and quiet setting, I couldn't help but gain some clarity.

For most of my adulthood, I had been juggling my work as a carpenter, my ever-draining bank accounts, and my relationships with my family so that I could follow my dream of traveling as a polar explorer. And I had been successful at it. My expedition teammates and I had been lauded in media and inscribed in the record books for epic feats such as skiing to the North Pole, circumnavigating Greenland by dogsled and kayak, and crossing the Bering Strait. If not for all those years of learning how to live in subzero deep freezes, I would have had no business being on Denali in the dead of winter.

Some people still thought I had no business being there.

I was somewhat new to climbing, and although my route on Denali wasn't a technically difficult one, with slopes of less than sixty degrees and little rock to navigate, it was more dangerous and required more technical skill than anything I'd ever undertaken. The mountain's weather is notoriously unstable, its altitude complicates breathing and thinking, and, of course, it presents a persistent threat of tumbling into oblivion. A few of my friends wondered if I was on a suicide mission, still grieving the end of my marriage.

Was I? I was hell-bent on completing this goal, maybe to a fault. But that is part of my stubborn nature. I relish the challenge of getting through difficult situations in extreme conditions with perseverance and tenacity. Once I start something, I can't stop until it is finished, putting myself in such situations again and again. In the case of Denali, maybe I was trying to finish this solo winter mountaineering feat to prove something to myself about who I was as a single man again. Out in the cold, among giant sheets of ice and piles of snow, I could make sense of my life more simply. In the vast frozen landscape, I felt at home. My human problems seemed less daunting.

With the dim winter sunlight waning and mountain winds pushing me around, the skiing was becoming increasingly grueling. *Shuffle. Shuffle. Exhale.* I wasn't sure how much longer I could keep going. My thigh muscles burned from the friction, the powder feeling more like sand with each stride. Through eyelashes iced over from my freezing breath, I could see the outlines of seracs to my right. The sharp-edged, dining-room-table-sized boulders of ice had cracked away from an icefall just above the ever-creeping Kahiltna Glacier. If one of those slid free, it would crush anything in its path. That would be a horrible place to set up my tent for the night.

To my left, at the base of a sharp, rocky ridge, the snow wasn't nearly as deep, but danger lurked just beneath it. Hidden crevasses—the large, gaping, seemingly endless holes in the ice that form in a glacier—threatened to swallow me forever if I hit one just wrong. Another bad place to camp.

I tried counting strides to stay focused as I forced myself to keep going. *One, two, rest. Three, four, rest. Shuffle, shuffle, exhale.*

At nearly 10,500-feet elevation, the skiing was getting harder, the altitude starting to rob my lungs of oxygen. *Five, six, deep breath.*

Finally, with the last of the sun glowing red on the horizon, I knew I had to make a decision. The safe spot where I wanted to camp was only about seven hundred more feet up the mountain, but if I had any real hope of getting there before total darkness, I had to shed some weight from my load.

Rounding a curve a hundred feet higher, smack in the middle of the steep gully, I stopped. I grabbed my eleven-inch aluminum mountaineering shovel from the packs in my sled, pulled out its telescoping handle, and started digging. I was going to bury part of my load, I decided, and I had to stash it at least three feet deep to protect it from being excavated by windstorms or raided. Even in that barren landscape, hungry ravens are looking for their next meal, the crafty birds capable of digging through snow and opening zippers. After twenty minutes of shoveling, I reached for the heaviest duffel bag on my sled—one filled with food and fuel—and pushed it into the hole. I'd need only my tent, my sleeping bags, and a few other supplies for the night, and I would ski fifteen minutes back down to get my buried cache in the morning.

I didn't worry much about the weather. The strong winds were gaining speed, but by Denali winter standards, the forecast had seemed decent when I talked to my expedition manager on a satellite phone a few hours earlier. I packed snow over the bag, then planted my black spruce pole next to it like a flag to mark the spot so I could find it easily in the morning. Focused on making my way to a safe camping spot, I didn't think twice about what I was about to leave behind.

It was a huge error that almost cost me my life.

Chapter 2

The Fledgling Explorer

I have always loved snow and ice. By the time I set foot on Denali alone in winter's depths, I had built up a lifetime of experience surviving and thriving in frigid temperatures. Cold was my specialty.

I got hooked on the wonders of winter as a young boy in central Minnesota. The blanketed white, frozen landscape offered a whole different world of beauty and challenge, and it energized me. I used to slide on my snow boots across frozen swamps to watch muskrats swim under a thick layer of ice. I followed the perfect paw prints of animal tracks through the pristine, glistening snow. I built caves in snowbanks and sledded down hills near our house.

Winter taught me to respect Mother Nature, too. At the tender age of six, my dad and I fell through the ice while riding his snowmobile over a frozen swamp. I remember his strong arms pushing me out of the icy water and onto the safety of the frozen surface. My wet snowsuit froze stiff as we raced home on the waterlogged machine, sharp pain throbbing in my freezing fingers and toes. It scared me as nothing else had in my young life, but it didn't deter me from embracing winter. I always wanted to see what was beyond the next snowdrift.

When I was fourteen, living with my mom and stepfather in a Twin Cities suburb, I convinced my stepdad to drive me and my friends Jay and Gary to a swamp about an hour north and drop us off to go winter camping on the day after Thanksgiving. I packed my bulky, flannel-lined Montgomery Ward sleeping bag. We grabbed muskrat traps, a few cans of food, and some leftover plastic sheeting from my stepfather's construction company. Then we crawled into the back of his red Ford work truck for a bumpy ride on a dirt road. He pulled over near the swamp and helped us unload.

"Pick you up Sunday at two o'clock," he told us.

We watched him drive away, the truck's rattling muffler fading to silence. Finally we were on our own, acting like rugged men.

We hiked through the woods looking for a decent place to make our shelter. I had developed some construction skills while working for my stepfather's business, so I served as foreman. We cut alder saplings with axes and nailed them together to form the frame of a lean-to, then stapled the plastic sheeting to the wood to form a roof and walls. I made a crude door using a couple of old hinges. We unfurled our sleeping bags on top of a few scrawny pine boughs that we foolishly thought would serve as good padding and insulation from the cold ground. Then we grabbed the muskrat traps and headed out onto the frozen slough.

We had almost finished setting up our traps when we heard a yelp and some splashing. The ice had cracked over by Gary, and he had fallen into water over his head. Jay and I scrambled over to him, slithering on our bellies as we got close and yanking him out by his arm. Inside our shoddy shelter, Gary peeled off his wet clothes and huddled in his sleeping bag, his teeth chattering. He hadn't brought a second set of clothes. None of us had.

We still had two days to go out there and no way to contact anybody for help, so we decided to try to keep Gary warm by eating. We tore into our stash of Oreo cookies, chips, canned pork and beans, and Slim Jim sausage sticks. We made a fire and roasted a chopped-up muskrat carcass I had brought in a mason quart jar to use as mink bait. It was a few days old and we questioned its freshness, but we decided the cooking would probably kill anything that would harm us.

At bedtime, Jay and I set our clothes in the corners of the shelter and tucked ourselves in, but we quickly learned that the pine boughs weren't nearly enough insulation to guard against the frozen ground of a cold November night in Minnesota. We were already shivering when it started to rain, then sleet. Our shelter leaked like a sieve; sheets of water blew in with every strong gust of wind. Everything got soaked. Then, when the temperature plummeted, everything froze stiff.

The next morning, we looked at each other, unsure what to say. We didn't know where the nearest neighbor lived, and we were in our long underwear, our soaked clothes now frozen, too. The wood, twigs, and pinecones on the ground were too wet to make a fire. As the wind continued to blow, we tried to cram our frozen clothes into any cracks in the tent walls to keep more snow from coming in. All we could do was concentrate on survival. We shivered in our soggy sleeping bags for hours on end.

Finally on Sunday, we heard the sweet sound of my stepfather's rattling truck coming to rescue us from the most treacherous weekend we'd had in our young lives. That disastrous trip taught us how quickly something can go wrong. Poor weather, an accident, or the wrong equipment can leave you vulnerable to the elements. But somehow the winter camping trip only inflamed my obsession with the outdoors. It sparked a challenge inside me to learn about how people lived in the world's harshest climates.

In high school, I devoured Foxfire books about living off the land, building log cabins, tanning hides, and foraging for edible plants. When my senior year rolled around and a guidance coun-selor pulled out a long list of possible occupations, I saw nothing that said "explorer" or "adventurer." I wanted to follow my passion in life, but how was I going to do that?

I worked for my stepfather after graduating because I couldn't find a better way to earn some money. But I was miserable pound-ing nails and taking orders from the bosses. As I drove home through slow-moving suburban traffic at the end of each workday, I daydreamed about living as an outdoorsman. I was determined to make that daydream a reality someday, and I grew afraid that if I didn't take a leap of faith to try it soon, I never would. I didn't want to stay forever in Plan B, working construction because it paid the bills. I was still young.

So, when I was only twenty-two, my cousin Dan and I loaded his camper-topped Chevy pickup full of cans of food and equipment and drove toward Alaska. We didn't have much of a game plan—just enough money to get us there if we slept in the truck along the way. We aimed to stay in Alaska for about three weeks and figured we would pick up an odd job or two to pay our way back. After spending the summer commercial fishing and living in a canvas, cabinlike wall tent on a remote bay, I was so enthralled with the state that I didn't want to leave.

I picked up construction jobs in Anchorage and, the next fall, my coworker John Petersen and I decided to go live in the bush for the winter. Over a couple of beers, we closed our eyes and pointed to random spots on a state map to pick the location of our new home:

the midpoint between where our fingers landed was wilderness just south of the Brooks Range mountains between the tiny towns of Bettles and Allakaket. We hired a pilot and loaded his Cessna full of food and supplies—a chainsaw, a woodstove, nails, plastic, and lots of other necessities as well as a few creature comforts. John wedged his tall, lumberjack-like frame in the front passenger seat, and I carefully sprawled out over our gear in the back.

We landed on the ominously named Deadman's Lake. The pilot agreed to come back and check on us at some point, but he didn't specify when. "Be careful," he warned us before he flew away.

John and I cut, notched, and stacked twiggy logs of Arctic birch to build an eleven-by-eleven-foot shelter. We had brought enough food for only about half the winter, so after we settled into our new home, we started hunting and trapping. We weren't as successful as we'd hoped. We made stew with the few rabbits we trapped, but the rest of our food supply was quickly dwindling. Fewer than sixty days into our adventure, in mid-December, we had little left to eat except canned fruit cocktail and extra-salty canned bacon. I shrank to the thinnest weight of my adult life. Our thermometer, nailed to a small tree behind the shack, read minus fifty-six degrees.

As December wore on, we saw no signs of our pilot. Finally, we decided we had to save ourselves.

In the first few days of January, we started out on a faint path in the snow, a snowmobile trail left by Athabaskan trappers. We estimated the village of Allakaket was about a thirty-two-mile snowshoe trek away. After ten spirit-crushing hours of taking turns breaking trail through thigh-deep powder, John and I stopped for the night, beyond hungry, dehydrated, and on the brink of total exhaustion. We shivered in our sleeping bags under the stars for a few hours, cradling our frozen cans of fruit cocktail in an attempt to thaw them for breakfast. We rose in the dark to continue on, icicles hanging from our eyelashes and beards. We were going to use an empty can to melt snow for drinking water, but we hadn't carried a stove, only matches and a couple cans of Sterno, which we had already used. We didn't want to waste time building a fire, so we drank very little. No moisture left in our mouths, our dry, crinkled lips cracked.

We stumbled on, my exhausted body working on autopilot as my mind told me nothing but *keep going.* I desperately wanted to lie down and sleep, if just for a few minutes. But I somehow knew I had to fight that overwhelming urge. If I fell asleep in the bitter cold malnourished and dehydrated, I would never get up.

The sun rose and fell again as we trudged. In the dark, John finally spotted light through the trees, and it seemed like the entrance to heaven. A woman who opened the door of a small cabin looked at us, aghast at the sight of our raggedy, sallow skin. She pointed us to the local school principal's house.

When we got there, John gulped about nine glasses of water, and I drank five or six. We may have been just hours from death. Our eyes were sunken, and our mouths were so cottony that we could hardly open them. After filling up on food from the school kitchen, we got a plane out of there and made our way back to Anchorage, broke and defeated. That spring, as Alaska's economy fell, I decided I had to get back to the lower forty-eight to make a living.

I didn't realize until after I left Alaska in 1986 that the whole time I was up there, I hadn't really gotten a good glimpse of Denali, then officially called Mount McKinley. Most of the time, the mountain is shrouded in clouds. On clear days, either I was too far away from it or my views were obstructed by other mountains. I knew North America's tallest peak was there somewhere, but I wasn't terribly interested in fixing my eyes upon it. I figured it probably looked a lot like the dozens of other majestic peaks all around me. I had no idea what I had missed.

When I arrived back in the Twin Cities suburbs, the local news was buzzing about an Arctic feat led by Minnesotan Will Steger. He and a team of explorers, which included fellow Minnesotans Paul Schurke and Ann Bancroft, had set off on an epic journey to the North Pole using sled dogs. I quickly grew engrossed in their story.

After one of their talks at the Midwest Mountaineering outdoor gear store in Minneapolis, I worked up the nerve to introduce myself to Steger and the others. I asked Steger about sleds, dogs, equipment, and funding. I also asked whether I might be starting out too late in life to be an explorer. I was twenty-five years old at the time. Steger grinned. My age was the last thing I needed to worry about, he said. Although he had gone exploring since he was a teenager, he hadn't led his first big sponsored expedition until he was forty. *I can relate to this guy,* I remember thinking. *If he can do it, I can do it.*

Getting to know the expedition members gave me confidence. I went to more of their talks and became fast friends with Schurke, who was courteous about answering my countless questions: What kind of clothing did they use to survive such cold temperatures? How did they figure out how much food and fuel to take? After I hung around with Schurke at his home outside the north woods town of Ely, Minnesota, we decided to go in on buying a team of nine pure Inuit sled dogs, creatures perfectly built for Arctic adventures.

Schurke was eager to take the dogs on his own expedition. Interested in global politics, he hatched an idea for a historic journey across the Bering Strait, the first diplomatic crossing of the border between Russia and the United States after decades of closure during the Cold War. Schurke invited me along, and I was beyond thrilled. I'd be traveling on an epic quest with one of my mentors. My dream of adventure was finally coming true.

Schurke and Russian Dmitry Shparo would lead ten of us, a total of six Americans and six Soviets, on a two-month journey stretching one thousand miles. We would use sled dogs as well as ski and briefly hop aboard a walrus-skin boat to cross the strait itself. Schurke worked the diplomacy angles and asked me to plan many of the trip logistics, including food, fuel, and equipment for humans and dogs. It was a lot of responsibility for someone so green, but I was honored. I relished the anticipation and the planning.

When we landed in Nome, Alaska, sixty-three days after starting the journey in Russia, I had a whole new sense of possibility. I knew then that my thirst for cold adventure was truly part of my soul. The expedition—officially named the Bering Bridge Expedition—was an incredible experience, immersing us in the cultures of indigenous people of the Bering Strait region. I got a chance to see and study their methods of thriving in an extreme climate.

On our way back to civilization, flying from Nome to Anchorage, I glanced out the plane window at what looked like an unusual formation of high clouds. Then my eyes adjusted. *Holy crap,* I thought. *That's a mountain.* It was my first clear look at Mount McKinley, or Denali, as Alaskans called it. It was startlingly massive. The sun was shining on its southern face, and it was illuminated more than the surrounding landscape. It looked like a beacon, high above all the other peaks.

I didn't know much about the many people who had climbed Denali by then. I had heard of only one man—renowned Japanese polar explorer Naomi Uemura, who had lost his life there several

Team member Darlene Apangalook, from St. Lawrence Island in Alaska, met her aunts from the Russian far east for the first time during the Bering Bridge Expedition. *Photo courtesy of the Bering Bridge Expedition*

years earlier trying to climb it alone during the winter. His body was still up there somewhere, among the jagged rocks and thick snow and ice. I thought about him as we flew past the mountain, and I wondered how he had met his end. Surely it couldn't have been the cold because the guy knew how to thrive in harsh elements. I wondered what had made him decide to climb in the first place.

Chapter 3

Cold Love

For the next two decades, cold expeditions became the focus of my life. I followed my passion of exploring the deepest freezes on the planet, crossing cultural barriers, and teaching the world about climate change.

I also reconnected with Kelly Bowden, a special education teacher I'd met on a winter wilderness camping fundraiser. She had surprised me with a letter congratulating me on the Bering Strait expedition. I was a father by then, recently divorced after a brief marriage to a city gal who, not at all interested in the outdoors, was a total mismatch for me. Kelly was different. We went hiking on our first few dates. Later, we went camping and canoeing in the woods of northern Minnesota.

Kelly's playful nature shined through her beaming smile, funny giggle, and big, sparkly blue eyes. She also understood my passion for cold exploration and even seemed enthused about being part of it. We got married in an apple orchard barn in December 1990 on a day when temperatures dropped below zero and a blizzard whipped up wind chills of minus fifty degrees. It suited us just fine.

Kelly helped me plan the first expedition that I would lead on my own: a three-thousand-mile, six-month dogsled trip across the entire length of the Canadian Arctic, from Alaska to Manitoba via the famed Northwest Passage ocean route connecting the Pacific and Atlantic. I wanted to learn more about the Inuit community, which I had glimpsed on the Bering Strait trip. How did natives of such cold lands survive? I recruited three men to make the trip with me.

Once we had secured enough money and supplies, I packed up my truck on a chilly October day and got ready to say good-bye to Kelly. We had been married less than a year, and the expedition meant we would not see each other again for months. Leaving her behind was heartrending, one of the hardest things I had ever done in my life. We loved each other so much, and yet we knew this was part of who I was. My need to explore was a driving force inside me, and if I denied myself that experience, I wouldn't be true to myself.

Outdoor adventures were filled with suffering and hardship, but by then I understood that for me, happiness came through effort and sacrifice. Rather than taking passive pleasure in easy luxuries such as dinners out and fancy hotels, I felt fulfilled by accomplishing something, by researching, planning, and trying to make a difference in this world through documenting climate change and the evolving culture of the Inuit people. Kelly was understanding and supportive, but we still had to pry ourselves apart, tears in our eyes, when it came time to say good-bye.

The expedition proved to be a great learning experience, both revealing new wonders and delivering tremendous hardship. We explorers followed the tundra's edge along the Arctic Ocean, a rocky, windswept, lifeless, and unforgiving place. When we reached the Alaska–Canada border, I felt strangely but profoundly connected to something intangible.

We were sliding by a half dozen abandoned old cabins that traders and trappers had built out of driftwood in the early 1900s. Nearby, a row of plank-shaped driftwood headstones marked a graveyard. It was like traveling through a ghost village frozen in time. I stopped at the makeshift cemetery and brushed the snow off a few of the markers, wondering about the lives of the people who had been in this remote place so long ago. One caught my attention in particular: "AИИIE," it read, with the NS written backward. She was just nineteen years old and had died on December 21, 1919, the darkest day of the year in one of the bleakest spots on the planet.

Several grave markers around hers listed the same year. Had some kind of illness swept through the village? That night, I dreamed about how scared and helpless Annie must have felt. The encounter with her grave stuck with me through the trip.

Our group of four explorers splintered as two headed home after a string of bad days. Continuing across the tundra, I stopped to rest my team of dogs at one point several weeks later, nothing but rock and snow and ice for miles around. I cinched my hood around my face to brace against wind-driven snow and walked up to check on the dogs. My teammate, Malcolm Vance, was doing the same a few yards ahead.

Suddenly, I felt a strange energy behind me, one that brought goose bumps up my spine and around my neck. *Shit*, I thought, stopping in my tracks. *Is it a polar bear?*

I turned very slowly to look all around, trying not to startle whatever it was. But I saw nothing. Still, I couldn't shake the feeling that something was near me as I continued to tend to the dogs. Out of the corner of my eye, I kept looking for whatever it was. Part of me fully expected that someone's hand would touch my face, either as a gesture of kindness or as a plea for help.

I went up to Malcolm and asked him, a little sheepishly, "Do you feel like someone else is here with us? I have the feeling someone is standing right next to us."

He looked at me, puzzled. "No," he replied.

"I do," I said, standing perfectly still.

"Have you ever felt it before?"

"No," I said softly. "Weird, huh?"

I've thought about that encounter a lot. Was it my mind playing tricks on me? If I had been cold, hungry, and run down at the time, I would have chalked it up to that. But I happened to be feeling pretty warm and satisfied that day. I wasn't under particularly hard stress as far as expeditions go.

In the months and years that followed, I mentioned this feeling to other explorers in casual conversations and found that most of them admitted to sensing something similar. I learned it was a phenomenon among climbers, polar explorers, and other people on extreme, dangerous journeys. Some attributed it to stress. Others figured it was their own alter ego revealing itself.

I'm not a religious man or even a very spiritual one, but I believe the sensation was the result of a sixth sense that everyone possesses but never uses in daily life. It becomes active only when we're void of distraction, in total isolation with our senses at their peak. When we're out in the wilderness for an extended period of time, we learn to focus on the present, to engross ourselves completely in our surroundings. Alone in nature's elements, we notice small details in order to survive on a most basic level. We look for fractures in the ice, we pay closer attention to the aches in our body, we scan for subtle changes in the sky to foretell the weather, we listen to every faint sound around us. Our ability to see, hear, smell, and touch is expanded. And if we're lucky, we can feel another dimension.

I know it sounds farfetched, but I always thought the fleeting presence out there in the Arctic that day was Annie. Whatever it was, I wasn't afraid of it. It brought me comfort, as if someone were watching over me.

I wanted to experience that amazing feeling again.

When I got back from the Arctic after so many months away, Kelly and I decided we had to find ways to include each other more in our life's passions. We immersed ourselves in a culture of the outdoors by moving to Grand Marais, a Minnesota tourist town on the shore of Lake Superior. A small community of fewer than fifteen hundred permanent residents, it swells with campers, hikers, paddlers, and cabin owners all summer long. It also has a thriving arts community, important to Kelly as she wanted to feed her creative side as a linoleum block cut artist.

During a 2006 North Pole expedition, we pulled canoes on skis across the Arctic Ocean. We left Ellesmere Island in Canada in May and reached the North Pole nearly two months later.

Kelly got a job with the local school district, and in between expeditions, I hustled to make money through construction. I decided I could have more control over my adventure schedule if I started my own construction business, so I put my planning and organizing skills to use by designing and building small log cabins. It wasn't a lucrative career, but it allowed Kelly and me to live simply in a 450-square-foot, run-down vacation cabin that we remodeled.

After a few years, I started planning the longest expedition challenge of my life: a journey with Australian adventurer John Hoelscher to circumnavigate Greenland by kayak and dogsled. Shifting sea ice around part of the country's perimeter is capable of crushing ships, so I wasn't too surprised to learn that nobody had circled its 6,500-mile coastline. The plan was to dogsled the northern part of the island in the winter and kayak the southern part in the summer, pulling our boats over melting ice floes if necessary.

After spending an entire summer kayaking on the island's west coast, we learned that we couldn't do the whole trip in one continuous fifteen-month shot. We hadn't planned for shoulder seasons, with unstable ice in the spring and fall, when it's impossible to safely kayak or travel by dogsled. Instead, the expedition ended up consuming the better part of five years of my life between planning, organizing, finding sponsors, and traveling back and forth.

Still, it was a highlight of my career. The mountainous shorelines and enormous icebergs of Greenland were spectacular. But most importantly, we learned about the northernmost inhabited place on the planet. From the Inuit people, we learned techniques for physically surviving deep freezes and mentally enduring darkness for months at a time. We learned how to be patient over the course of so many years. I was enthralled and passionate in Greenland, living my true calling. But every day I was out there, I knew I was missing something back home.

My son, Jacob, was just eleven years old when we set out on the trip's first leg. I missed big blocks of his life over the next five years as he grew from a child into a teenager. I was gone for three spans of six months or more, and during that time, it wasn't easy to communicate with anyone back home.

Most often, I reached Kelly through a sixteen-pound radio we carried but could use only when we came across a scientific or military outpost, which was about once a week. I spoke directly to Jacob only a few times and inevitably heard the heartbreaking, guilt-inducing question, "When are you coming home?" On those days, I wanted to beam myself back to Minnesota like the characters on *Star Trek.* I hoped that someday while pursuing his own dreams, Jacob would look back, forgive my absence, and take inspiration from what I'd done.

The Greenland trip, like all the others, proved tough on my marriage, too. It was hard for Kelly to live on her own for so long. At that point we resided on forty acres of woods northeast of Grand Marais in a log cabin without electricity or plumbing. It was a mile on foot—hiking, snowshoeing, or skiing—to get in and out. Kelly was also caring for a dozen of my unruly sled dogs and wild puppies. I felt like a schmuck at times, trying to straddle my passion for the wild and my deep love for my wife.

Through many of my expeditions, Kelly and I wrote gushing love letters to each other. At one point, I wrote a list of ways that I would improve, ranging from small deeds such as putting the cap on the toothpaste to larger commitments such as promising I would go for long walks with her every day and spend more time with Jacob. I accomplished parts of my list, but truth be told, no matter what I did at home, it was hard to make up for such long absences.

Kelly was outwardly encouraging about my trips, including subsequent expeditions to the North Pole, saying she was proud of me for living my dreams and doing what I was meant to do. "I knew who Lonnie was before I married him, knowing what I was getting into," she would say. But I knew, underneath it all, she was riding a roller coaster of happiness and emptiness. She couldn't help but worry about me. She knew I didn't take foolish chances, but she also knew that if I got stuck in a dangerous situation out of my control, there was nothing she could do about it.

I don't think anybody—me included—really understood the intensity and longevity of my need to explore. Both Kelly and I were hoping that my inner drive for adventure would fade and that we could live a more normal life someday. Dreams and passions of the young often morph into something more mainstream. Mine never did.

In the summer of 2009, I took a 125-mile solo canoe trip into the Quetico wilderness of Ontario, Canada. It was a way for me to clear the bugs off the windshield of my life and see things more clearly. It was also the first journey I took completely alone.

I wondered if I would flip out and start having conversations with myself. Very few people are alone for more than a full twenty-four-hour day. In a way, the trip was a personal test. It taught me that I could survive on my own, deciding everything by myself. The time among the lakes and trees, undisturbed by others or by distractions from life on the grid, also gave me a chance to think clearly about who I was and what I wanted. I came out the other end no worse for wear, though I told my friends, with a smile, that the company hadn't been the greatest.

That fall, after nearly twenty years, Kelly and I dissolved our marriage. It was the most agonizing time in my life. It wasn't fair to either of us to continue together with my leaving her behind so often. Kelly might have explained it best when she once wrote, "Isn't it strange how sometimes one of the things you love most about a person is also the very thing that causes the most hardship?"

Our divorce crushed me. For all of my adult life, I had never really been single, at least not for long. For two decades, Kelly had provided a solid base for me and my lofty exploits. The thought of her got me through a lot of hardship on my trips, knowing I had a strong foundation back home. Suddenly it was gone.

Part of me felt adrift, floating solo with no land in sight. I was pushing fifty years old and found myself searching for meaning again. For so long I had been "Kelly's husband." Who was I now?

Chapter 4

Denali Calls

Reeling from the end of a twenty-year marriage, I turned to my friends to dull the sting.

Many Friday nights, I would meet my pal Buck Benson, a Grand Marais businessman, for a glass of Malbec at the Raven Pub, a local hangout. We'd sit at the same small round table in the dark barroom just a couple hundred yards off the harbor, fishing net and ceramic figures of pirates hanging from the walls around us.

Buck is single and athletic, a strong, blond Swede who appreciates a good joke. He had run ultramarathons, bicycled long distances, and skied in Nordic races. He'd also hiked quite a few mountains, making it to the top of several 14,000-foot peaks in Colorado; Africa's highest, 19,341-foot Mount Kilimanjaro; and the 22,841-foot Aconcagua, the highest in South America. Buck's mother had recently died, and in between talking about the big transitions in our lives, he threw out a harebrained suggestion, knowing we needed a break and a good challenge: we should climb Mount McKinley.

I shrugged off his idea. Neither of us had any technical climbing experience. I was an Arctic explorer, not a mountaineer. I reminded

Buck that the highest thing I'd ever climbed was an apple tree on the farm where I grew up—and that it hadn't been easy. Mountain climbing had never appealed to me. I didn't know of too many climbers who lived to a ripe old age. No matter how good they became, I thought, all it took was one bad step. Sooner or later they would slip, and their number was up. Plus, I'd always thought climbers were conquering mountains solely for themselves—"peak bagging," some people called it—triumphing over nature to gain fame with little value to the rest of the world. I also didn't see a lot of exploration in it. The climbing community was relatively large compared to Arctic explorers. I figured all the interesting, accessible peaks had been climbed.

But the more I thought about it, the more I realized I needed a change at that point in my life, even if it was just for myself. Doing something completely different started to appeal to me. And with all of life's complications, I wanted the simplicity of focusing on a single feat—no sponsors to solicit, no audience watching, no media expectations. Just surviving with food, water, and shelter. Just putting one foot in front of the other.

Finally, after a few months of joking about it, I raised the idea with Buck for real.

"Maybe we should do that," I said as we sat at our table in the bar one night.

I already knew that Buck was a good travel companion. He had paddled a two-hundred-mile section of the coast of Greenland with John and me, and he'd kept a positive attitude, a trait I had come to prioritize in any expedition partner. Buck had told me that if I ever invited him on another trip, he'd jump at the chance.

We started to think about who else we might recruit to climb with us. I looked no further than my roommate. Tom Surprenant, who had hiked peaks in Colorado and run ultramarathons, was a longtime friend through our shared interest in the outdoors. With his bald head and snow-white beard, I always thought he looked like a reincarnation of Gandhi but slightly more handsome. He was also going through a major life crisis. An information technology professional, he had been between jobs and lacked health insurance when a mountain biking crash left him with seven broken ribs, collapsed lungs, and eventual bankruptcy. On top of that, he was going through a divorce. We had moved in together in a small house in Grand Marais, two guys in a fog of doubt, trying to figure out our new lives. I knew Tom didn't have money for a trip at the time, but I also knew he needed the journey more than Buck and I. I loaned him the funds, hoping it would give him the confidence to rebound emotionally as well as physically.

My friends Buck Benson (left) and Tom Surprenant (middle) were climbing companions on my first attempt at Denali.

We also invited a friend of Buck's, Steve Pitschka, an emergency physician who lived a couple of hours away in Duluth. In his forties, he was fit and strong as an ox. He would serve as our climbing team doctor.

We would call our trip "Mount Denial."

Looking back, we were all naïve about what we were getting into.

We wisely decided to climb in June during regular climbing season, but perhaps stupidly, we decided to try it without a guide. With all my cold weather experience, we figured we already had half the battle won. I knew that with a little research, I could figure out our basic gear and food. Buck secured our permits for the most popular route up the mountain: the West Buttress.

We researched what we would need for mountaineering equipment. Denali isn't considered a technical climb; we wouldn't need to scale sheer cliffs or cling to a wall by the tips of our fingers. Still, it required a lot of careful treading between crevasses atop snow and ice at high altitude. It was far more technical than anything any of us had ever done.

We ordered the appropriate ropes and carabiners to secure ourselves together. We learned about running belays—in our case, a technique to drive metal stakes into the snow and slip our team's rope through an attached clip for extra security on steep slopes. We learned about ascenders, small mechanical devices that attach to a fixed rope, sliding only in one direction to secure us when ascending a steep incline.

We learned that Denali has more vertical feet of climbing from base camp than Everest, even though its peak is some 8,700 feet lower in elevation. Its location on the planet near the Arctic Circle makes the conditions extra difficult. Sitting north of the Gulf of Alaska and east of the Bering Strait, it gets pounded by violent

storms that can last weeks at a time. By some estimates, Denali's
20,310-foot summit is akin to an elevation between 21,000 and
23,000 feet on another mountain.

The more I learned, the more I became intrigued. The challenges on a high mountain were different from those in the Arctic.
We would be traversing steep slopes prone to avalanches and crossing glaciers with deeper crevasses than I'd ever traveled around.
Staying warm at altitude is also more difficult, with less oxygen
in the blood to fuel circulation. I'd even need to tweak my Arctic-
perfected menu as the altitude made it more difficult to digest fat.
All those differences motivated me. It would be an entirely new
challenge.

We trained for the climb in the spring, several months before
the trip. I started with short runs, bike rides, and a mix of core and
upper body exercises. Later I ran hills. As a team, we hiked several
hilly trails near Lake Superior with weighted packs. At one point,
I filled a pack with fifty pounds of road salt, strapped it to my back,
and hiked up and down a 179-step outdoor staircase near a waterfall
called the Devil's Kettle. I tethered a tire to my body and dragged it
up a hill behind Grand Marais.

We flew to Anchorage in early June and hopped a shuttle to
Talkeetna, a tight-knit village of about nine hundred residents,
perched on the Susitna River south of Denali National Park. About
sixty air miles from the mountain, the town serves as a home base
for climbers who get ferried up to base camp through one of a handful of ski plane companies. Talkeetna's downtown is only a few
blocks, with Nagley's general store on one end and a National Park
Service office on the other. In the middle sits the Roadhouse, a 1917
log hotel and restaurant that we used as our base for last-minute
preparations and relaxing before our climb. Talkeetna is jokingly

The famous Talkeetna Roadhouse—our in-town base camp, where we could eat, sleep, shower, and manage expedition logistics

known as a drinking town with a climbing problem, and it's a great place to meet like-minded adventurers over a beer or two.

Before flying to base camp at 7,200 feet on the Kahiltna Glacier, we took a one-day class at the Alaska Mountaineering School called Denali Skills Workshop. In our case, they could have called it Denali for Dummies. It was a crash course designed specifically for that mountain. We learned how to maneuver our feet in crampons, the sharp metal spikes attached to our heels and toes, to help us climb steep slopes of snow and ice. That meant learning various footing techniques, including walking flat-footed like a duck and plunge-stepping, digging in our heels on the way down. We had to consciously avoid getting the crampons snagged on our pant legs, potentially sending us flipping head over heels.

We learned how teams work together to cross Denali's glaciers, linked by rope through waist harnesses. The instructors also taught us how to self-arrest—to swiftly use our ice axes to stop ourselves if our footing slipped. Yell "Falling!" to our teammates, they told us, and thrust our axes as deep as we can into the snow and ice. They spoke as if it were commonplace to use a small piece of metal to stop from plummeting off a mountainside and into oblivion.

The instructors also taught us how to rescue one another from a glacial crevasse, which on Denali could be hundreds of feet deep. From afar, those cracks look like ripples. But the instructors assured us that up close, the narrower ones are sometimes snow-covered and undetectable. They can devour a climber. Buck and I looked at each other and laughed nervously. We were truly green in the world of mountaineering. After one day of instruction, there was no way we would remember all the detailed steps to rescue someone from a crevasse. But we figured that among the four of us, we would have enough ingenuity to improvise. Better yet, we decided we just wouldn't fall into a crevasse.

Personally, I wasn't insistent on summiting. In my mind, we would just use our common sense and my cold weather expedition skills to have fun up there. If the climb became too difficult, we'd just turn around. I was there for the adventure and the challenge. I wanted to hang out with the guys, sleep in a tent, tell some stories, and soak in the incredible views. Learning to climb would be a bonus.

Chapter 5

Mount Denial

On a clear day, panoramic views of the Alaska Range are among the most breathtaking sights on earth. Sharp, rocky peaks jut through blankets of crisp white snow. It's the kind of scenery that makes a person stop and gaze in amazement that something so beautiful is naturally part of our planet. The mountains are rugged, rough, and majestic. They are perfect.

Even amid all that grandeur, Denali stands out, a snowy behemoth stretching wider and nearly three thousand feet higher than its tallest neighbor. It dominates the skyline.

While the mountain was officially named Mount McKinley in 1917 after the US president, locals and climbers had long called it Denali, which is derived from native Athabaskan languages and roughly translated as the "tall" or "high" one, according to linguist James Kari. The federal government finally agreed to officially change its name to Denali in 2015 after years of lobbying from the state and others.

As we flew out of Talkeetna and our airplane floated low over the shorter mountains in the vast range, I thought about all the remote peaks and valleys that had probably never been climbed, the places that had never been touched by humans. Maybe there was more to explore in mountaineering than I had thought.

The Talkeetna Air Taxi plane took us through One Shot Pass, a large bite out of a mountain ridge. It felt as if the wing tips might brush the rocks as we banked through the opening leading to the forty-four-mile-long Kahiltna Glacier, the longest sheet of ice in the Alaska Range. A colorful sea of other climbers' tents greeted us when we landed on the glacier, and I felt the pang of nerves in my stomach. This trip was for real.

We had come during the peak of climbing season, and the mountain was bustling. After so many expeditions across the Arctic, I found it jarring to see so many other humans in such a remote place. The park permits fifteen hundred climbers from April 1 to August 1, though most try to scale the mountain in May and June, when conditions are most favorable and success rates are typically highest. Early-season climbers face colder temperatures; late-season climbers face more danger from crevasses after a summer of warmth.

As many as five to six hundred climbers might be on the mountain's West Buttress at its busiest times, and some high camps can be crowded with as many as a few hundred people. The park service has mountaineering rangers stationed at various spots along the route, and in one spot there are fixed ropes for climbers to clip into. Still, the park service emphasizes that each team of climbers should be prepared to be self-sufficient. Though climbers had been scaling the mountain for nearly a century, beginning with native Alaskan Walter Harper and his team in June of 1913, the overall success rate typically hovered around half.

I wondered which half we would fall into as we unloaded the airplane. I was feeling strong and optimistic. We would be setting out on skis, each carrying heavy loads of supplies. We would have packs on our backs and sleds tethered to our torsos. In wide-open areas, we would be marking our path with a set of four-foot-long bamboo wands with little flags of red duct tape stuck to the top so we could find our way out in case of low visibility from a storm or clouds. We had a satellite phone with us as well as an emergency locator beacon in case of trouble.

As we organized our gear among the buzz of people and planes coming in and out of base camp, we made small talk with some of the other climbers, but like them, we were mostly focused on prepping for the journey ahead. We buried and marked a cache of food and fuel to use on our return. Then we set out, strung together by a two-hundred-foot rope, onto the crevasse-filled glacier.

I set the pace from the front. Throughout the trip, I would strive to find the sweet spot of moving fast enough to make good progress but slow enough to satisfy the most tired among us. It would be a constantly adjusting equation. We let the rope sag between us just a little, keeping it loose enough so we could each move comfortably but taut enough that if one of us fell into a hole, he wouldn't fall far.

Following the tracks of other climbers, we carefully wove our way across the glacier's latticework of deep crevasses. Some were huge and obvious, their deep holes darkened to midnight blue and black, but many others were hard to detect because of snow blanketing them. They were the most dangerous, hidden but still big enough to gobble climbers.

The first day, we made it a few kilometers across the glacier without much trouble, first down a slight incline and then all the way to the upper Kahiltna, to 7,800 feet. From there, the glacier steepened as we worked our way up on the second day. We wanted to get to 9,700-feet elevation, where we were told we'd find a good spot to camp.

The conditions were warm. Though it was great to be traveling in twenty-four hours of daylight, we were walking on snow, and the air around us was misty, limiting visibility. The summer sun glared brightly right through the mist and reflected off white terrain all around us. We shed our warmest clothes, feeling as if we were in a microwave with the rays frying our exposed skin. We covered our faces in thick sunblock, wore brimmed caps, and kept bandanas draped over our necks. We had to concentrate to keep track of our footing in the sea of white snow and ice. Besides that, we were starting to feel the altitude, our breathing growing slightly strained to bring in enough oxygen.

The whole climb seemed to be taking longer than I thought it should. As we approached camp and saw tents in the distance, something didn't seem right to me. I had studied a map of our route ahead of time, anticipating what we would see at each point in our trek. I was expecting a broad basin where the upper Kahiltna widens, but instead I was looking at a narrow corridor with a hill to the north. We had also veered east right before seeing the camp.

"I think we're at 11,200," I said.

"Nah," Tom said. "Couldn't be."

Tom checked an altimeter he was wearing on his wrist. Sure enough: 11,200 feet. A team camped a few yards away confirmed it. How had we completely missed the 9,700 camp and made it all the way up there? *Oh well,* we thought. Our progress was great. At least there was no doubt about our fitness levels. We were tired but feeling pretty good as we settled into our tents for the night, Tom and I in one and Buck and Steve in another.

We were looking forward to resting there for a day before switching from skis to crampons to climb the steeper terrain ahead. But the next morning, our momentum came to a screeching halt when Buck announced that Steve was sick. Steve had woken Buck at 3:00 AM after monitoring himself and finding that his oxygen levels had dropped critically low. Steve was nauseous and a little incoherent, confused about what he needed to do. He couldn't communicate very well.

Steve diagnosed himself with altitude sickness. I was surprised by that. We weren't that high on the mountain. But we had ascended quickly, and people's bodies respond differently to such conditions. I felt Steve should wait a bit, drink fluids, and rest, letting his body adjust to the thinner air. But Buck consulted with Steve, and he wanted to go down. Tom agreed.

It was a crushing development. We had worked our butts off to get that high on the mountain, and now we would have to descend and do it all again. It was as if we were getting kicked before we even got a good start. I thought about suggesting that we pull the plug on the trip. I don't think anybody would have argued against that idea at that moment. But I didn't actually say anything about quitting. Buck and Tom didn't either. We left part of our supplies at the 11,200-foot camp and headed back down.

The conditions had turned dangerous. Blowing snow on the mountain meant little visibility and a good chance that we could get lost. Any tracks left by us and other climbers had been covered, making us more vulnerable to dangerous crevasses. But we needed to evacuate Steve. We'd heard all kinds of horror stories about what can happen with altitude sickness—people coughing up blood and going into a coma. We didn't want to take any chances. Steve was a doctor, and if he decided it was best for him to go down, we were going to take him.

Tom and I tied into each end of the rope, with Steve and Buck in the middle. We followed our wands as we headed back down. When I couldn't see the next wand ahead of us, I stopped and Tom kept moving at the other end, our rope tight, until he found the wand. From above, it would have looked as though Tom were a pendulum. We had to repeat that pathfinding technique for most of the day.

Steve started feeling better as we descended. As we rested in our tents that afternoon, he continued to improve, feeling even better in the morning. But he didn't want to test fate. He called off his trip. We had prepared to accompany Steve all the way back to base camp, but when we talked with another team heading down, Steve agreed to descend with them.

Then there were three.

As Buck, Tom, and I climbed back up to 11,200, everything went smoothly. Most people leave their skis and switch to crampons at that point, but we were cross-country skiers from Minnesota and thought we would try to herringbone our way up a steep eight-hundred-foot slope with our skis so we could move faster. It was a rookie mistake. Halfway up, we had to stop. It was impossible to walk like ducks, pointing our long skis at angles, while pulling heavy sleds up such steep terrain. We took off our skis and skittered up the crevassed slope in our boots until we could reach a spot where we could dig out our crampons.

After watching other climbers, we learned that depending on the weather, it might be better to climb at night, when the sun sits low on the horizon and snow bridges across the tops of crevasses are frozen stronger. It would certainly be cooler at night, a good thing at the lower elevations. With twenty-four hours of daylight, we didn't need headlamps up there, even in the darkest hours.

As we climbed higher on the mountain, though, we had to be able to quickly add more layers of clothing. You could go from sweating in the sun to freezing in the shadow of the mountain within minutes.

When we reached a technically difficult spot on the mountain at about 15,000-feet elevation, I started to wonder what it would be like to climb Denali on my own. Not tethered to anyone, I wouldn't have to worry about falling and dragging my teammates down with me or getting yanked off my feet if someone else slipped. Being tied to each other gave us a sense of security, but if one of us fell and we couldn't self-arrest, we would all be dragged down together, with our only hope for not tumbling to our deaths being the rope catching on the jagged rocks below.

We used fixed ropes that the park service had installed to climb up the headwall, a roughly nine-hundred-foot, fifty-degree slope of snow and ice that felt similar to the steep roof of an A-frame cabin. We kicked the toes of our crampons into the terrain carefully from 15,000- to 16,000-feet elevation, heavy packs tugging on our center of balance. The climb killed our calf muscles. We kept trudging, moving next along a ridge that rose steeply and was boot-width narrow at points with long drop-offs on both sides.

Then, just eleven days after we started, we made it to the West Buttress high camp. At 17,200 feet, it's the traditional spot where climbers rest and wait for good weather before shedding most of their gear and setting out for a long day's push for the summit. It's dangerous to try to camp higher than that point. Storms are more likely, it's more difficult for climbers to stay warm in the thin air, and the winds blow harder at that elevation. There are also very few places to dig down into hard-packed snow to set up a tent. So we made our camp near four other teams and a group of climbing rangers at 17,200 and settled in.

We got to meet mountain-climbing legend Vern Tejas, who was camped next to us. The first person to climb the Seven Summits of the world ten times, Vern at that time was working as an extraordinarily credentialed guide for a group of climbers. He was close to his fiftieth summit of Denali and had been the first person to survive a solo winter summit of the mountain, which he had accomplished in March of 1988.

We knew that a summit attempt would test our physical and mental limits. It would require more than a three-thousand-foot elevation gain, and we would have to travel extremely light to move at a fast enough pace.

We woke up to sunshine after a night of heavy snow. With a fresh, thick layer clinging to the mountain, we worried about our footing and the possibility of avalanches on our first one thousand feet in elevation gain, a snowy and icy slope that climbers call the Autobahn. That section of the mountain has seen more fatalities than any other and is purportedly nicknamed for German climbers who met their demise there.

After consulting with another team and giving the snow some time to settle, Buck, Tom, and I decided to go for it. We ate our morning staple of granola with goat milk and then filled ourselves with liquids, including hot cocoa. We set out about 11:30 AM carrying a minimal amount of supplies.

We slogged hard through the Autobahn, roped together and scrambling slowly and steadily, not stopping even for gulps of water. For extra safety we used a running belay, where I, as the first person heading up the mountain, would pound a picket into the snow and slide our rope into a carabiner attached to the picket. After we all passed it, the last person would take the picket out. It was nice to come across and use a few extra pickets already up there, pounded in by other climbing teams and park rangers.

When we finally sat down in the snow for a break at 18,000 feet, digging in our crampons to keep from sliding, we each pulled out our one-liter Nalgene bottles of water and drank about half. We realized then that we probably should have brought double the amount of water that we did. I mentioned to Buck and Tom that we would have to pick up our pace if we wanted to make it to the summit, let alone back down to camp. Especially at its higher elevations, Denali is known for sudden storms and biting cold winds that have killed entire climbing teams. The faster we could summit and get back down, the better.

As we continued to climb, I grew concerned that we were moving too slowly. We knew it took most parties twelve or thirteen hours to go from high camp to the summit and back. The way things were going, we would need several more hours. The terrain wasn't technical, so that wasn't the problem. I wasn't sure why we were falling behind our faster-than-average pace. But I knew we couldn't afford to be caught up there in a storm without sleeping bags or tents and without a way to melt snow into water.

At 19,000 feet, we stopped to regroup and Tom sat down to rest. I was still feeling fine—my body and state of mind more accustomed to long endurance expeditions—but I could tell that both Buck and Tom were struggling at times. They were more conditioned for half- and full-day races. By that point, I had been pushing them a bit, prompting them to move faster than their comfort range. I wondered if they were feeling frustrated trying to keep up.

Just then, Buck suggested that we split up and travel at our own paces. It would be our own decision to go for the summit. He told me to go on ahead. I agreed to keep moving while Buck and Tom continued to rest a while longer. Before I took off, I reminded myself and them that there would be no shame in stopping. Summiting North America's tallest mountain is an epic feat even in the best conditions during peak climbing season.

It was closing in on midnight by the time I approached the ridge just west of Denali's summit. At that altitude, about three hundred feet below the top, I was moving extremely slowly in such thin air.

There was no worn path up there, the wind quickly erasing the tracks of other climbers. I took small steps on the ridge, trying to stay away from the cornice, a hardened, windblown snowdrift shaped like a wave curling over the edge of the ridge, nothing but a mile of air underneath it. I kept my ice axe in my right hand and used it as a probe, poking its handle into the snow for support and to make sure there was still mountain underneath me. At one point, it poked all the way through. My heart skipped a beat. I quickly but smoothly shuffled sideways, down a few steps, and back onto the safety of the ridge.

As I slogged in about minus twenty degrees Fahrenheit, every baby step required a rest and two deep breaths. Every strike of my foot required a conscious effort to make sure my crampons were firmly dug into the windblown surface of ice and snow.

Finally, up ahead, I saw it: a small metal disc sticking out like a pinhead from the cushion of snow and ice on the small, bulbous top of North America. "U.S. DEPARTMENT OF INTERIOR," it said. "UNLAWFUL TO DISTURB."

I had made it. I breathed a sigh of relief and paused to consider how fortunate I was to be standing there. But mostly I was in awe of the view. Even then, near midnight in late June, the sun was shining on the top of Denali, casting the giant mountain's shadow onto low-lying clouds to the north. What an extraordinary view.

I slowly spun in a circle to look in every direction. The peaks of the entire Alaska Range poked through the clouds and clear spots below me. The mountains that had loomed so tall from base camp now appeared dwarfed. In the distance to the south, a carpet of dark forest stretched for miles. It was a moment I would remember forever. Standing up there on top of North America, I felt incredibly lucky and humble. All the hardship had been worth it.

I snapped a few photographs and slowly turned again to get the full view one more time. Then I told myself it was time to go. I still had hours of dangerous travel ahead of me, and I was worried about Buck and Tom.

Watching my steps on the ridge back down, I was surprised to see two figures coming up about five hundred feet below. My buddies were still moving and were getting so close to the top. I was elated for them. But I was worried, too. I'd had more energy than they did, and I felt exhausted. How could they summit and still have enough gumption to safely get back down?

I stepped faster, and when I saw Buck approaching, I dug my crampons into the ground, planted my ice axe, and knelt to wait for him. "Buck, be careful!" I warned, my mind now heavy with worry. "Are you sure you've got the strength to go up and come back down again?"

He didn't look good. But he said he felt good, and he was determined to continue. My instincts told me it was a bad decision, and hearing him say it made me emotional. "You really need to hurry," I told him, tears welling in my eyes. "We're running out of time here because we've already been pushing longer than we should have been."

Tom and Buck heading up the West Buttress Ridge

Who was I to make him turn around? Buck had more experience with altitude than I did. He was an adult. We were on this expedition partly as a team but mostly as friends. I couldn't stop him, but I worried. I had the same conversation with Tom, who was not far behind Buck. I reminded each of them that we still had a long, dangerous descent to get back to camp.

Hesitantly, I kept heading down the mountain. I stopped when I got to a spot at about 19,200 feet. I had to wait for my buddies.

I stayed there for what seemed like an eternity, pacing back and forth, trying to stay warm. Cold crept into my bones. I had a shovel with me in case we needed to dig an emergency snow cave for shelter, and I decided to use it in case Buck and Tom were too tired to keep going. At least we would have a somewhat protected spot. But the snow was rock hard. I couldn't break through its crust with the shovel. I tried picking at it with my ice axe, but that didn't work either as I heaved it twice between gasping for air. I grew more worried as the minutes ticked by, wondering what kind of trouble my friends were in above me. I was so tired, but I wondered at what point I should go back up for them.

Finally, after more than two hours, I saw them creep down the mountain. I was so relieved. When they approached, I could see they were exhausted. Tom staggered slightly as he stepped. But I knew it would be dangerous for us to rest. We had been at high altitude far longer than most Denali climbers, and we needed to keep going.

About a hundred feet below, we stopped again, and I pulled our communal thermos of bouillon soup from my pack and unscrewed the lid. We gagged at the lukewarm, salty, oily brine. We just couldn't drink that stuff. I was experiencing for the first time how altitude can affect a person's palate. The thought of eating anything made my stomach turn. None of us wanted the soup, so I figured I could shed its weight from my pack. Without thinking, I just poured it out. Looking back, I should have insisted that we drink the soup, but I was new to climbing and didn't understand what was happening at the time.

"Come on, you guys. We *have* to go down right away," I said. I clipped a rope onto them, and we pushed hard as I led our small pack.

Most fatalities happen to mountaineers who are descending, with good footing more difficult to see at the same time momentum carries them forward and down. We knew it was especially true on the Autobahn, where summiters are tired and prone to mistakes. I was extremely careful about where I stepped, and I kept my axe pointed toward the mountain, ready to drive it into the snow. Every step of the way, I imagined one of us slipping and pulling the whole team down.

As we neared our tents at 17,200 feet, we were all spent. We had been on the trail at high elevation for nineteen hours straight since leaving high camp. Most expeditions take twelve to thirteen hours to summit, but because we had to break trail through deep snow and hadn't hydrated enough, it had taken us much longer.

Before any of us slept that night, we all drank as much water as we could. We still couldn't even think about eating, but at that point I didn't care. We needed to stop ourselves from becoming debilitated with dehydration. Our eyes were dry, our tongues were tacky, and our already chapped lips were cracked.

Vern, whose team was still acclimating at 17,200 feet, told us he had been worried about us during our whole trip to the summit, but he congratulated us on making it to the top and said he was glad we hadn't tried to rush on our descent. It was a nice affirmation coming from such a climbing superstar.

Denali wasn't finished teaching us lessons, though. On the way down a couple of days later, Buck got a good, long look at the inside of a crevasse.

We had left our camp at 14,000 feet and headed off the plateau into a part of the route where glacier ice had bent and split apart, creating monster crevasses that seemed bottomless. We were treading carefully, and I glanced back at my team periodically. At one point, I saw only Tom.

"Where's Buck?" I asked just as I felt the rope behind me go tense.

Tom and I simultaneously and instinctually pulled forward. We realized right away that Buck must have fallen. We hoped he was only on the lip of a crevasse so that we could just pull him out by continuing to move ahead. But he had fallen in too far. He was hanging by our rope, his pack on his back and his sled dangling from his waist, gravity tugging him down.

To Buck, the fall felt more like a drop, the ground giving way underneath him, he said later. It had happened fast, and there was nothing to grab, no way to stop himself. He was lucky that he hadn't been injured, hadn't hit his head on the hard ice walls or broken a limb. Initially, in fact, he tried to climb up the rope to get out on his own, but he soon realized that was ridiculous, he said, so he just decided to relax. He knew we would rescue him— eventually. So he waited inside the crevasse, where it was eerily silent and still.

Luckily, another climbing group was just passing us heading up the mountain, and their guide sprang into action to help us. He managed to get right up next to the crevasse, where he bent down, grabbed a handful of rope, and pulled it up and out while Tom and I continued pulling. Slowly, we were all pulling Buck out, inch by inch. It took about twenty minutes.

Once Buck got out and was back up on his skis, he waved to us that he was okay. We breathed a sigh of relief and continued moving. Buck had put a lot of trust in the rope and our ability to pull him from that hole. We were lucky that it had worked so easily.

The whole expedition had gone remarkably well, really. The three of us had completed our trip in just thirteen days, including taking Steve partway down and then coming back up. In hindsight, that detour helped the three of us acclimate better. We had made the trip to the top of the continent far faster than the average of seventeen to twenty-one days. We were strong, and we had had good weather and good luck.

I didn't realize how fortunate we had been.

Chapter 6

Thinking of Going Alone

Back in Minnesota, having forgotten about our hardships, I couldn't stop thinking about our climb and my newfound interest in mountaineering. I tried to figure out how I could combine that new type of adventure with my first love: cold.

Denali offered plenty of that.

I studied a mountaineering booklet from the National Park Service, and it didn't hold back on warning about Denali's foreboding weather, even during the summer. It included a book excerpt from medical doctor Peter H. Hackett that called the mountain's intense cold one of its unique features and compared it to Antarctica. "The Himalaya is tropical by comparison," Hackett wrote.

The park service warned that from November through April, average temperatures on Denali ranged from minus thirty to minus seventy, recorded at the 19,000-foot level. The jet stream, with winds of over one hundred miles per hour, often descends on the mountain's upper regions in winter, the booklet explained. With the "venturi effect" doubling wind velocity in some areas, "you will find one of the most hostile environments on this planet. . . . Winter climbing in Denali borders on ridiculous," the park service advised.

"Some of the world's best climbers have either disappeared or perished from literally being flash frozen!"

I was not surprised that when I researched attempts to scale Denali in winter, I learned there hadn't been many. Only sixteen people had summited Denali in the winter according to the National Park Service. Six climbers died from their winter attempts. Almost all who had succeeded in wintertime climbs did it in the slightly more temperate and daylight-filled weeks of late February and March. Three American climbers—Art Davidson, Dave Johnston, and Ray Genet—were the first to reach the summit in the winter, accomplishing it in late February 1967 as part of an eight-person

In December 2014, just before my fourth solo attempt at the summit, I visited with Dave Johnston, who had summitted Denali with two fellow climbers in February 1967. *Photo by Bob Marshall*

expedition. Their teammate, French climber Jacques "Farine" Batkin, was killed early in the trip after falling, unroped, into a crevasse. Davidson recounted the mountain's hostile environment in his book *Minus 148 Degrees*. He described a fierce storm that forced him and the two others to hole up in a small ice cave for six days above 18,000 feet while descending. Other members of their party, who had been socked in about a thousand feet below, eventually left them for dead.

Nobody ascended in winter again until the 1980s according to park service records. In March 1982, two out of a three-person team summited. In March 1983, one of two summiting team members died on the descent. Only two climbers, Russians Artur Testof and Vladimir Ananich, successfully summited during the month of January, reaching the top on January 16, 1998. A third member of their team came out alive but did not summit.

Traveling in teams was dangerous enough in winter. But solo climbing at that time of year was a whole different story. Naomi Uemura, the Japanese polar explorer, made the first winter solo ascent of Denali in 1984. Like me, Uemura had a wealth of experience in the cold. He had traversed the Arctic by dogsled from Greenland to Alaska and had gone to the North Pole alone. Unlike me, Uemura also had a lot of mountaineering experience. He had climbed the highest peak on every continent except Antarctica. He reached the top of Denali on February 12, 1984, at age forty-four and made national news for his feat. But his luck ran out on his way down. A snowstorm blew in as he descended, and he was lost somewhere between 18,200 and 16,000 feet.

Four years later, Vern Tejas became the first person to solo summit successfully in the winter and return safely, reaching the top amid clouds and falling snow at about 4:30 PM on March 7,

1988. In honor of Uemura, he planted a small Japanese flag at the summit.

Two other climbers solo summited in winter after that: American Dave Staeheli made the first solo winter ascent of the West Rib route in March 1989, and Japanese Masatoshi Kuriaki made it to the top in March 1998. Kuriaki had been the last person to even attempt a winter solo ascent, and that was more than a dozen years earlier.

The park service booklet admonished climbers against solo travel anytime on the mountain, explaining that even the most cautious and experienced had trouble detecting the location and strength of snow bridges over crevasses. "Virtually all experienced Alaska Range mountaineers are not willing to accept this level of risk," the booklet said before stating at the bottom of the page in bold capital letters, "WE STRONGLY RECOMMEND AGAINST SOLO TRAVEL."

In all my research, I found that nobody had ever summited Denali alone in January in the midst of the darkest and coldest days the winter could produce. It seemed like a good challenge for me. I already knew how to handle dark and frigid days, and the mountain's climbing route was fresh in my mind. Solo winter mountain climbing could be the next chapter in my life, but I didn't want to rely on Internet research to figure out the best way to attempt it. I knew from my polar exploration that real insider knowledge isn't always publicly available.

I found an email address for Tejas and wrote to ask his advice. He was friendly and generous with recommendations, and I was grateful. You never know how other adventurers might react to such requests. Vern went out of his way to answer some likely annoying questions from a fledgling mountaineer. It probably helped that we had heard of each other before meeting on Denali in 2010.

My Arctic travels gave me credibility in the relatively insular world of outdoor adventurers. I had survived a fifty-four-day expedition to the North Pole when temperatures started at minus fifty-eight degrees and never rose above minus twenty-two degrees, and I had endured sixty-four days of polar night traversing the Northwest Passage. Tejas knew I was serious and that I could handle cold and dark conditions. Plus, my attempt wouldn't usurp his accomplishment. He was the first human to successfully solo climb Denali in winter, and nobody could change that.

Tejas emailed me with his thoughts. "Wow, dead of winter! You do like a challenge. Short days and hard to route find in the dark," he wrote. "We both have a warped sense of what fun is."

At Vern Tejas's suggestion, on my first two solo attempts I took a ladder with me for protection against falling into crevasses. On subsequent trips I used poles, which were lighter and less cumbersome, instead.

He suggested I bring a ladder, as he had done, to prevent fall-ing into a crevasse. He added that he had taken two types of ice axe, which he said would be "nice if you did survive a crevasse fall and had to climb out." He also suggested preacclimatizing so I could move faster and lighter, either by climbing another mountain in the Southern Hemisphere right before heading to Denali or by using a special altitude tent as Olympians do. He also warned me about the conditions. In the dead of winter, he wrote, it might not snow as much because it's so incredibly cold and dry at that latitude and altitude. I would be traversing hard and icy slopes, and I would need the right equipment to stop myself from sliding off the moun-tain. "At least 2 winter climbers likely died not self arresting falls," he wrote.

Artur Testov, part of the team that summited Denali in January 1998, was also generous with recommendations, telling me that if I hoped to reach the top starting from a camp at 17,200 on sum-mit day, as most climbers do in peak season, I would have to travel extra light and swiftly. "Just remember," he wrote, "night comes quick and weather changes super fast in the winter."

Chapter 7

Making It Happen

I didn't want to wait too long. With the West Buttress route still fresh in my mind from the summer climb, I decided that I would try for a solo winter summit right away, a mere seven months after I first set foot on the mountain.

But even though I had just been to the summit, I knew I needed to cram to learn more about mountaineering and altitude if I were to go it alone. I'd have no teammates to help me, so I would need to be especially prepared. It would require extra diligence on the mountain to keep myself from plunging into crevasses, to stop myself should I start sliding down a steep incline, and to watch myself for signs of illness and hypothermia.

Thinking about who could help me train for it all, I remembered a particularly engaging guide we'd met on our summer Denali climb. We had made a connection on the mountain, partly because his wife happened to be from Minnesota. I thought he might make a good instructor, but I couldn't remember his name. With some Internet sleuthing, I tracked him down, recognizing his photograph: Elías de Andrés Martos. He worked as a guide for RMI Expeditions, a climbing and trekking company based in Washington

State. He was certified with the American Mountain Guides Association in mountaineering and ice and rock instructing. I emailed him to ask if he would help me train, and when he said yes, I latched onto him as my guru. If I weren't cut out for a winter solo mountaineering quest, I was counting on him to help make that clear to me.

I flew to Colorado, where Elías liked to climb, and he gave me crash courses on ice climbing, footwork, and all sorts of self-arrest techniques. We concentrated on the facets of mountaineering that were specific to Denali's West Buttress route and to climbing solo. At one point we practiced on a double-black-diamond ski run in Aspen at 4:00 AM, before the slopes were flooded with snowboarders and skiers. I learned to trust in my crampons. I learned to listen for the hollow sound my ice axe made when it hit ice too weak to hold me. I learned to keep three points of contact on the mountain at all times. We also practiced dry tooling, which is using crampons and ice axes to climb rock. I learned to cling to rock faces using cracks just a half inch deep. It was a skill I didn't expect to need on Denali, but I wanted to be prepared in case I found myself in a dangerous situation.

Perhaps most importantly, Elías taught me to think quickly about how I would save myself when falling from every possible position: What's my move to self-arrest while falling on my back? How about falling on my face? Falling to the side? If I were to get going sliding on my butt, I learned, I should not dig in with my crampons; I would risk breaking a leg when the spikes bit into the surface and tumbling down face first. Instead, I learned to lift my crampons, dig in my ice axe using both hands on my side, and flip onto my stomach on top of the axe. Occasionally when we were training on the mountain, Elías would surprise me with a shove, his way of

Learning to use and trust in my crampons was an essential lesson in mountaineering. I used fourteen-point crampons to keep me in contact with the mountain during my Denali climbs.

testing me so I could practice stopping every type of fall I might encounter.

In between climbs with Elías, I worked on my skills back home in Grand Marais, drilling the lessons into my head so they became second nature. I was preparing and practicing for anything and everything that could go wrong, and it all made me realize even more how lucky Buck, Tom, and I had been climbing on our own.

I spent a lot of time researching also to determine the optimal combination of supplies and food. Weight, warmth, and quality were key. I would be pulling and carrying everything I needed to sustain me. I needed the warmest and lightest climbing gear I could find, and that requirement was more difficult to fulfill than I'd imagined. Most climbers shy away from super-cold temperatures, so there isn't a market for ultrawarm climbing gear. Many of the clothes I wore on Arctic expeditions were simply too heavy or too stiff for climbing. It was just the opposite for footwear. The soft-soled, roomy, and warm moose-hide mukluks that served me so well on a dogsled wouldn't work with crampons. Climbing required stiffer, more supportive mountaineering boots.

I ended up modifying a lot of my gear. I bought a pair of Boreal climbing boots several sizes too big so I could stuff my own warm liner system inside them. I placed rubber waffle-weave material in them as insoles to capture moisture from my foot. Then came a synthetic felt insole, a thick synthetic snowmobile boot liner, a big puffy wool sock, a medium PrimaLoft sock, a vapor barrier liner, and finally, next to my foot, a thin merino wool sock. I made sure the boots were flexible enough to keep my circulation yet supportive enough for dangerous terrain.

As for my clothes, I was happy that I could incorporate a lightweight mix of PrimaLoft and goose down into my layers, something that didn't work on many of my other expeditions when humidity from Arctic sea ice threatened to seep into the feathers. Once down is wet, it's useless for warmth. The mountain would be a much drier environment.

I also recalculated how much white gas I would need for my stove based on altitude, and I refined my food menu to give me the most concentrated and useful calories for the weight. In the Arctic, I took food that was high in fat; at altitude on Denali, I would need more carbohydrates and protein. My food and fuel would weigh the most, so I wanted to take the lightest amount possible while staying assured that I would have enough.

On a polar expedition, I took as much as a liter of white gas per person per day to help combat the extreme cold, heat the tent, and dry clothing from the humidity. The drier mountain meant I wouldn't need to carry as much for the latter, and I would take food that required very little cooking. After talking with other climbers, I concluded I could get by on about seven ounces of fuel a day.

I had to get everything just right. I couldn't bring much spare gear because it would be too heavy to schlep. I had to think about ways to tether equipment or stake it down so it wouldn't fly off the mountain. If I dropped my shovel or if any piece of gear flew away in hurricane-force winds, it would be game over.

I also had the big task of figuring out how to pay for my climb. After so many Arctic expeditions, I had built up relationships with sponsors, though it had taken many years of trial and error and rejection. I always felt uneasy walking into plush boardrooms to speak to representatives from big international companies. I had to become sort of a chameleon, turning myself from an outdoorsman who preferred sleeping in tents on barren sheets of ice into a businessman making presentations and negotiating deals.

I had figured out that it helped to choose projects that benefited society in some way—contributing to scientific research or educating people about another culture or climate change. It also helped when projects were unusual or novel enough to garner attention. My mountain quest fit that latter category. Nobody was going to pay someone to climb Denali in the summer because it had been done so many times. But a solo winter quest would be notable and worthy of sponsorship.

Fortunately, going solo on Denali was relatively inexpensive compared to the Arctic expeditions I had undertaken. Greenland had cost more than $600,000, and the North Pole totaled about $375,000. I could climb Denali solo for less than $10,000.

I turned to sponsors, selling the solo climbing expedition in the best way I knew how. "This is a personal challenge of mine," I told them honestly. "I want to test the skills that I've learned over the years, and I want to learn more about myself and how I do in a solo situation." Then I explained what was in it for them. I found the circulations and rates for a full-page color advertisement in popular adventure magazines; then I showed them statistics on how many people had followed my previous expeditions on social media and through other coverage. Our summer North Pole expedition in 2006 reached millions of people, for instance. Unlike a magazine ad, I would actually be using the sponsors' products in extreme conditions, giving them more authentic exposure to more people, I explained. And I would be willing to do it for a fraction of the price of the magazines. "It's a real scenario, so it's a much better bang for your buck," I told them.

I ended up with major sponsorships from PrimaLoft and Granite Gear, as well as smaller sponsorships from others. Truth was, I was so determined to attempt a solo winter climb of Denali that I would have found a way to go even if I had to use up my own savings.

My friends could see my passion for the trip, and they questioned my obsession. Climbing solo was more dangerous than anything I had done, some reminded me. They wanted to know why I was so hell-bent on it.

"Why are you switching to climbing?" they asked, probing gently, trying to delve into my psyche. "That never really appealed to you. Why are you taking it up now?" They wondered if my reaction to my divorce was pushing me hastily into a foolish quest.

They wondered why I was suddenly willing to take on so much more risk.

True, I didn't initially have any interest in mountaineering, I told them. But after I'd set foot on Denali, I realized that climbing held new challenges and mountains contained immense beauty up close. I had never realized there were so many mountains that hadn't been explored, so many places and ways that I could learn about other cold landscapes on this planet. It was also a chance to learn about myself in a different way.

"I know the seriousness of it," I told my friends. "I'm not jumping into this thing blind." But I didn't spend a lot of time trying to convince them. I let them think what they wanted.

They worried quietly and wished me luck, telling me, "Don't go get yourself hurt."

None of us knew that my solo Denali quest would consume me for four years.

Chapter 8

Try, Try Again

For three winters in a row, I subjected myself to the cold danger of trying to solo Denali. In all, I spent more than sixty days on the mountain in the months of December and January, discovering how temperamental Denali could be: sunny and inviting one day, stormy and foreboding the next. The mountain seemed determined to thwart me, but after each try, I adjusted my plan and gear to help improve my chances for success.

On my first try, I couldn't even get to base camp for ten days. I had arrived in Talkeetna just before New Year's Eve and was stuck, a bundle of nerves and excitement, waiting for stormy weather to clear. I had all my gear packed, and I had gone through all the logistics with the park service office in town. The rangers there knew from my past expeditions that I was a professional when it came to extreme cold and that I had climbed Denali that summer.

Their main concern—rightly so—was that I would be traveling alone over glacial terrain. They asked how I planned to avoid crevasses and how I would get out if I fell into one. They also grilled me about my emergency plan and my communications equipment, wanting to know the names and phone numbers of the people I was going to contact. They were thorough in their instructions and as helpful as they could be, giving me their assessments of last-known snow conditions and crevasses at various spots along the route. Then they asked where I planned to camp and the specific colors of my clothing in case they needed to search for me.

Finally, the weather cleared on January 7, 2011, and I was ready for takeoff. As the plane flew up above the snow-covered forests and mountain peaks, I thought about what it was going to feel like to be dropped off at base camp by myself. Would I be able to hold myself together up there with no one to talk to, without anyone to consult? As we flew farther away from Talkeetna, the feeling of isolation heightened.

After unloading all my gear and hugging my pilots good-bye, I got an especially eerie feeling watching the plane fly away. I was utterly alone in such a harsh and desolate place. Looking around and overhead at the cathedral of mountains surrounding me, I felt powerless and insignificant. Part of me wanted to climb into my sleeping bag and wait for the plane to come back. What was I thinking by taking on this challenge?

I ended up lucky that first trip. I climbed all the way to the high camp at 17,200-feet elevation quickly with no major problems. The temperatures hovered at about minus thirty-five degrees, as I knew they would, but the short days were clear enough for me to keep moving. I somehow found a way through every difficult and scary obstacle. My equipment performed well. I felt strong and in shape. And even though I had ascended quickly by most standards, I didn't get hit with altitude sickness. I pushed myself to exhaustion, but I was having great success.

Then all the snafus seemed to hit at once.

I reached the 17,200-foot camp two and a half hours after dark, after fourteen hours of climbing. I had pushed hard to get there, knowing I would rest for a day or two while waiting for good weather before attempting to summit.

I hadn't bothered to carry a tent with me that year. I knew from experience that digging a shelter in the snow and covering it with a roof made of large, thick-sawn snow panels would be warmer anyway. The only catch was that snow shelters took a lot of time and effort to build, especially at altitude. I mustered all the mental strength that I could to override my physical fatigue and dug a small snow shelter for the night. It was 10:30 PM by the time I collapsed into my haven at 17,200 feet, my energy spent.

I lived in this snow trench at 17,200 feet for almost a week during my first solo attempt in 2011.

I woke up to a pounding headache. The quick altitude gain from climbing three thousand feet the day before was catching up with me. A couple of ibuprofen helped.

Everything in my shelter was covered with a half inch of snow, blown in through the small vent hole I had punched in the roof and other tiny openings that I couldn't close. A storm had roared in overnight. It was minus thirty degrees outside and minus five degrees in my cave according to a small thermometer I had brought with me. It was the coldest I had ever felt that trip.

I tried to start the stove, first releasing a bit of raw gas to prime the burner as I had always done. But this time it didn't work. As I flicked a lighter to start it, the stove caught fire, and so did my liner gloves and the plywood I used for a stove base. I tossed the stove to the front of the cave and jammed my flaming hands into the snow wall. Flailing around in my tiny hovel, throwing snow and contorting my body, I finally snuffed out all the flames. I was lucky that I had no burns on my hands, but my liner gloves were toast. The chemical scent of burnt synthetic permeated the whole cave. I realized that the extreme cold had shrunk the O-rings in the stove's pump assembly, allowing gas to leak out. I'd had a similar problem on a North Pole trip, but I hadn't spotted the leak this time. I should have warmed the pump over a candle or under layers of my clothes before starting the stove. It was a lapse of judgment from my oxygen-deprived brain.

The storm didn't relent, and for days I could hear the whistle of the wind and the *thunks* from plates of hard snow flying across my roof. Denali was showing me her cruel side, snapping into a rage and pinning me down so close to the top.

After four days of lying cramped in my tiny burrow, the down in my sleeping bag clumped into little feather ice cubes. Aiming to lighten my load high on the mountain, I hadn't brought my sleep-ing bag vapor barrier or outer sleeping bag with me, deciding I would sleep in more clothes to keep warm. But perspiration from my body condensed into my bag, and its insulating qualities were diminishing fast. It wasn't nearly warm enough anymore.

It was miserable, and then I felt the scary sensation of my shelter shaking violently, floors and walls, for a good fifteen seconds. Snow chunks fell from the ceiling as I crouched deeper into the hood of my sleeping bag. *Shit*, I thought. *Must be an avalanche.* But then I thought about it. An avalanche wasn't likely at that spot on the mountain. I peeked out of my cave toward the Autobahn and saw no evidence of a massive snowslide.

Eventually, I figured that it had to have been an earthquake. I later learned that it was a 5.4 on the Richter scale, its epicenter just a few miles north of me in the foothills of the range. It was an amazing, creepy feeling to realize, all alone up there, that the earth has enough inner power to shake North America's tallest mountain so much. I shook my head and had to chuckle. In all of my detailed preparations, one thing I hadn't planned for was an earthquake.

As the storm raged on, I occasionally got up and out of my den, and I could feel that my muscles were starting to atrophy. My arms and legs felt skinny and weak. I felt lethargic; getting up and out of the cave took too much effort.

At one point, as I started to consider the disheartening question of whether I should head back down, I rearranged my supplies to take stock of what I had. Before I knew it, a full fuel bottle fell out of a bag, and I watched it tumble down, down, down the mountain like a slow-motion scene in a movie as I cursed aloud. I expected the bottle would vanish, but I saw that it came to rest on a frozen wave of snow about one hundred yards away and about fifty feet lower in altitude. I stared at it for a minute, then took a deep breath. If every ounce of fuel hadn't been absolutely precious, I would have left that canister behind. But I could see it, and it was within reach. I mustered up the energy in my shaking limbs to carefully crawl down to retrieve the bottle, chiding myself the whole way for letting it slip and tumble in the first place.

After five days and six nights at my 17,200 camp, the high altitude and low temperatures were taking their toll on my mind and body, and I was running low on food and fuel. The weather had improved, but a cloud was still shrouding Denali Pass, my route to the top. A bid for the summit was not going to happen. Instead, I took a lull in the storm as my signal to retreat.

I reached base camp lightly battered and bruised, and greatly humbled. Denali hadn't allowed me to reach its summit on my first winter solo try. It wouldn't allow me to pass so easily. I was disappointed to turn around after getting so close to the top, but in all my years of expeditions, I had learned that there was no shame in calling it quits. A wise explorer doesn't let ego get in the way. He or she knows when to quit in order to travel another day and when to go back to the drawing board and tweak the plan.

Twelve months later, I was back on the mountain. Again my climb started out relatively easy. I made it all the way to 15,000 feet with supplies, then camped at 14,200 feet without any major incidents.

Building a snow shelter is always an ordeal, but by then I had refined my process to its most efficient form. I dug a roughly four-foot-by-four-foot cube out of the surface. Then I carved out a space on one side to extend my legs when lying down. That was my sleeping platform. Next to the platform, I dug a fourteen-by-eighteen-inch space where I could put my legs so I could sit comfortably. Then I used a snow saw to cut six to eight thick snow panels that balanced against each other to make a peaked roof, great for headroom when sitting, which is key to being able to spend days in a shelter if necessary. In the peak, I made a three-inch vent hole to let fresh air in and the stove exhaust out.

I was comfortable in my haven when a blizzard swooped in. I spent seven days and six nights in that little cave, periodically scraping the walls and ceiling of the icy glaze that forms from body warmth, stove heat, and breathing. Freshly built shelters are porous and dry, but after a few days of human habitation, the walls turn to ice, and the cave becomes colder and damper with no dry snow to soak up the humidity. Living in such tight quarters makes even the simplest of tasks a major undertaking. It was a constant battle to keep snow from falling onto everything as I moved around. With so many belongings crammed inside with me, it seemed to take forever to find a lost mitt, fill a thermos with hot water, or contort myself to answer nature's call.

Finally, on the seventh day, my expedition manager confirmed in a satellite phone call that wind gusts had reached ninety-seven miles per hour, but the forecast called for a lull. Feeling weak and battered once again, I decided to head down when the storm let up a little. On my descent, wind gusts shoved me like a bully, pushing me over and over as I struggled to stay upright. At 12,600 feet, the wind knocked me off my icy balance. I tried to walk flat-footed so all fourteen points on each of my crampons could grip the surface. My quad muscles strained as I faltered down an icy incline, a fifteen-hundred-foot drop at my side. When I heard the next big gust coming, I hit the deck, swinging my axe into the ice and bracing my feet. I stood up again with a wide stance, using a ski pole for balance as I continued down.

Another sudden blast of wind caught me off guard, throwing me face first down the hill. I felt my body pick up speed, and I immediately went into a self-arrest. I swung the pick of my axe to one side, penetrating the hard surface and slowing my fall. Momentum carried me about fifteen feet more down the hill before I finally stopped. I lay there on top of my axe, panting and trying to compose myself. *Don't stand up. It's too windy,* I told myself. For the next two hours in the darkness, I slithered down the mountain in a push-up position, using my crampons and axe to cling to the surface. It was exhausting work.

Denali still wasn't done kicking my ass.

The next day, when I was just a few hours from base camp, a blizzard descended again, socking me in once more. I pulled out my shovel and started digging a shelter, but after chopping through the top layer of snow, about two and a half feet down, my shovel made a sharp *thuck* noise and sent a jolt of pain to my elbows. I had hit marble-hard ice. There would be no digging through that. I went about one hundred feet away and tried a different spot. Same thing.

The wind was almost blowing me off my feet again. I finally found a small drift of snow and decided to dig a notch into it from the side, hoping the top would stay in place and give me a little bit of shelter. I just needed a spot to hunker down. But for every shovelful of snow I dug out, the wind blew three-quarters of it back in. The snow spinning in the air filled my mouth every time I took a breath, almost choking me.

I got down on my knees and started pulling the snow away with my arms. Finally, the hole was big enough to fit my foam pad and sleeping bag inside. I wedged myself in and pulled the sleeping bag over the top of me, not even bothering to crawl inside of it. I pulled my backpack up to the wide opening on the side and huddled there behind it, stuck in the fetal position and worried I might not survive. I tried to brush away all the snow that had flown into the cuffs and creases of my clothes, worried I might get hypothermia if it melted.

My beard was encased in a thick coating of ice from nose to chest, and I felt that I was starting to suffocate. In a panic to get more air, I grabbed the edge of the beard ice and yanked on it, ripping a four-inch sheet from my face along with whiskers and some blood. It stung like hell, but I was relieved that I could take deep breaths again.

Exhausted, I managed to eat some cold food and drink the contents of my thermos. Then I passed out. When I woke up in the middle of the night, it was dead silent. I shoved the backpack out of the way, poked my head out, and saw bright moonlight illuminate all the peaks around me.

Finally, it was clear. I could make it back to base camp and get the hell off the mountain.

~

When I came back the next year for my third solo attempt, Denali tried to smack me down earlier than ever. I was camped at just 9,200 feet when menacing skies dumped nearly eight feet of snow on me over the course of thirty-six hours. I came dangerously close to succumbing to the elements.

I had dug out my snow shelter for the night and stretched a tarp overhead to make a roof, as I had planned to do on all my shelters

During my second solo attempt, the estimated wind-chill temperature was minus sixty degrees as I prepared to camp at 14,000 feet.

that year. With the snow falling heavily, I tried to catch a few winks of sleep. I was afraid to snooze too long, though, worried that I would be permanently buried, so periodically I got up to shovel snow off the roof.

After a couple rounds, I woke up feeling short of breath. I opened the tarp door above me and saw only snow, and I realized my roof's three-inch vent hole was completely plugged. I started digging overhead, and with every shovel scratch, snow fell into the cave, where I stamped it down with my feet. I dug and dug, stamped and stamped. I couldn't believe how much snow had accumulated above me. I was buried. It seemed endless, and I felt a wave of panic but tried to remain calm.

I grew exhausted from keeping my arms raised while scraping with the shovel above my head, and I was soon soaking wet, too. My shelter was filling up with snow, but I had yet to break the surface. Finally, as I stood on the tips of my toes, my arm extended as high as I could reach, the corner of the shovel finally broke through. Fresh air rushed in, and I filled my lungs with deep breaths of relief. The bitter cold never tasted so sweet.

I spent the next hour mucking out my cave and digging my gear out from under the snow. Once the work was over, I started shivering. Then I shivered violently. I felt my heart racing and my whole body trembling. I was confused about how I had gotten to that point. Over all my years of Arctic travel, I thought I had developed an astute sense of what my body needed. I knew when to hydrate, when to pull on another jacket, and when to swing my arms to get blood flowing to my fingers. An explorer has to pay close attention when help is so far away. But I had missed the signs this time.

Nearly eight feet of snow fell in just two days during my third solo trip. I had to climb out of my shelter periodically to make sure my gear was not getting completely buried. I was also badly in need of fresh oxygen.

"Warm up! Warm up!" I tried to command my fifty-one-year-old body. I put on as many clothes as I could, adding a down vest and parka to my two layers of hoodies, long underwear, and insulated pants. I wedged myself into my sleeping bag system and drank warm water from my thermos. I poured the rest of the warm water into a Nalgene bottle and tucked it against my bare chest, trying to use it like a heating pad. I stuffed my mouth with chocolate, like cramming firewood into a stove. I worried I was too late in trying to stop my downward spiral.

Then I must have passed out. I woke up several hours later, unsure at first where I was. I was no longer shivering, but my heart was racing, and I struggled to breathe. I checked my pulse: over 120 beats per minute.

I noticed my vent hole was plugged again, too. I crawled out of my cave, but the snow was too deep to walk around much. Still, the fresh air and stretching made me feel better. My pulse dropped back to 55. I was relieved to be alive and humbled by my vulnerability. I had seen—and almost crossed—the delicate line between beating heart and corpse. The whole ordeal had shaken me to my core. It also made me long for a way to sleep above ground, where I imagined it would have been less damp.

I was out of danger with no debilitating injuries, and the weather seemed to be clearing. There was no reason not to continue. I just needed to take it slow to get my energy back. I dug into some of my extra food, eating four servings of macaroni and cheese for dinner one night, trying to stay warm. The next night, I ate four servings of mashed potatoes with peas. It seemed to help. I willed myself to keep going.

When I finally reached high camp at 17,200 feet, I had developed a rattling, fluid-filled cough. My throat produced yellow phlegm, and my wheezing got worse. I had developed a mild case of pulmonary edema—altitude sickness resulting in fluid on my lungs. I had been feeling run down and might have climbed faster than my tired body could handle.

The forecast called for seventy-mile-an-hour winds, which sealed my decision to retreat. I used two ice axes to scale down the steep sections and made it back to my 14,200 camp, coughing my head off but safe.

Some people say it was courageous to turn around so close to the summit. Maybe so, but I was also being realistic and weighing the odds. I was confident I could plow ahead to the summit but equally sure I would perish on the descent. Making it to the summit is optional; making it back down is mandatory.

I left Denali short of my goal for the third year in a row.

~

It was disheartening, of course. My first three attempts had meant three years of training, organizing, fundraising, and hardship. Three years in a row, sponsors had shelled out money to support my efforts

People ask if I get disappointed when I don't reach my goal on an expedition. Sure I do. Deciding when to turn around can be excruciating, but often the answer becomes obvious because of the weather or dwindling supplies. Explorers learn quickly to make peace with Mother Nature, to work around her rather than try to fight through her. When I make the call to retreat, I don't worry about disappointing anyone else. Friends, family, and sponsors all want me to live. I chalk it up as a learning experience that will make me better.

I know I can go back someday. Denali is not going anywhere.

Chapter 9

One More Try

Shortly after my second and third attempts at soloing Denali, I had told myself that I wasn't going back. I figured my luck would eventually run out and Denali would kill me. I thought going back meant asking for trouble.

When winter rolled around again in late 2013, I gave Denali a rest. I went climbing and hiking in Colorado and spent time skiing at home in Minnesota, something I had missed. But over time, a person forgets the hardships. Climbing Denali solo in January was unfinished business, and it was eating at me. I didn't want to grow old saying, "I wish I would have done that."

I kept thinking of the expression, "Fear regret, not failure." I was already feeling regret. I had come so close to success up there, and I thought about more tweaks I could make to my strategy and my equipment. *Next time I'm going to wear different clothes so I don't get hypothermic,* I'd tell myself. Or, *I'm going to take a different set of skis.*

I enjoy planning expeditions, but after so many years spent on one goal, the fun was starting to wane. I wanted to put the solo winter summit challenge behind me and move forward. Sometimes, a guy has to push himself. So in mid-December 2014, I once again found myself climbing aboard an airplane to Denali's base camp.

I rode in a 1950s Beaver with a Rotax engine as it floated low between mountain peaks. As we circled above the landing spot, Talkeetna Air Taxi pilot Paul Roderick opened his side window and threw out a black plastic garbage bag weighted with a small rock. Then he dumped another. And another.

Roderick, a thirty-year veteran flying the wilds of Alaska, was marking a runway on the Lower Kahiltna Glacier. Dropping bags is a trick pilots use up there when the winter sun is so low that it casts no shadows and it's extra difficult to judge depth. The black bags atop the white snow gave Roderick a visual reference of where to land safely, distinguishing the flat spot from a slope and giving him a sense of our altitude. It was a rare clear day, but Roderick had only a short window of sunshine on the narrow slot between the mountains where he could land. At that time of year, Denali sees only about five hours of daylight.

"I've got the butterflies now," I told an Anchorage TV reporter who was on the flight with us to document my launch. "But having butterflies is good because that little bit of nervousness keeps you alive."

It was about 1:45 PM when the skis on the plane cut through the soft blanket of snow, bobbing and spraying puffs of powder to the sides. When we came to a stop in an amphitheater-like spot at 7,200-feet elevation, we had no time to waste. As soon as the propellers stopped, Paul opened his door and jumped out to cover the plane's engine with a thick blanket, attempting to keep it from freezing solid in the short time it would be grounded. Although he always kept emergency survival gear in the plane, he didn't want to get stuck there waiting for help.

Paul donned snowshoes to retrieve the bag markers and to pack down a runway six hundred yards long for the plane's skis to get speed and lift in the deep snow. I unloaded the plane and then dug a three-foot-deep hole in the snow to bury a cache of supplies: an extra sleeping bag, an extra tent, and a ten-day supply of food and fuel in case winter storms prevented the plane from picking me up at the end of my trip. I marked my stash with several twelve-foot bamboo wands, each adorned with small flags of black duct tape and reflective silver tape so I could see them if I was traveling by headlamp, as I often did in winter.

After landing at Kahiltna base camp in December 2014, I went off to establish a cache of supplies for my return, while pilot Paul Roderick used his snowshoes to pack down a runway for his departure. *Photo by John Walter Whittier*

I packed the rest of my gear and food into my sled and hoisted a full pack onto my back. With my five-foot-six-inch frame, I was dragging and carrying more than 190 pounds of stuff, the equivalent of another person far larger than me. I was also at my heaviest. I had packed on a few extra pounds anticipating that I would lose about fifteen on the mountain, as I had on each previous trip. Just before I left Minnesota, my mother fed me a hearty meal of barbecued ribs, baby red potatoes, and homemade coleslaw.

My Granite Gear backpack contained an emergency kit: a satellite phone, a tiny stove, a couple of days' worth of food and fuel, two ice axes, an emergency locating transmitter, and extra batteries for the headlamp. Two sleeping pads and a shovel were strapped to the pack. The sled, attached to my waist with a rope harness, contained almost everything else: nearly a month's worth of food and fuel, extra layers of clothing for the higher and colder altitudes, a spare satellite phone, a homemade battery pack to charge electronics, 175 bamboo wands, crampons, and other gear for the climb that lay ahead.

Attached to my custom Boreal mountaineering boots with telemark bindings were special eight-foot-long, four-inch-wide wooden skis that I had cut myself from yellow birch trees on my Minnesota property. With the help of a good friend, I had formed, steamed, bent, and epoxied the wood.

I also attached my spruce pole to my torso with strong climbing rope. The thirteen-foot-long, three-inch-diameter tree trunk—one I had chopped from a dead tree in the woods near Talkeetna just before flying up to base camp—was heavy and cumbersome, but dragging it along would be worth it to stop my fall into a crevasse. I'd be traversing the giant holes from there up to 14,200 feet. I needed the safety insurance.

I had taken an aluminum ladder on my first two trips, but I decided it was too heavy. Aluminum poles, which I took on my third trip, were too cold and slippery. I liked the idea of a spruce pole, bringing the smell of pine and the feel of wood to the mostly lifeless landscape.

As Paul got his plane ready for takeoff, I braced myself to set off on my fourth solo attempt to summit Denali in the dead of winter. Even I briefly questioned my sanity at that moment. All the excitement, energy, and anticipation that go into planning such a trip were beginning to fade as I stood there once more at square one.

"I never think past day one. I just do one day at a time. This is my job," I had told the TV reporter, putting on a brave face. "It's just like going to work, right? Only I like it."

I hugged my pilot good-bye. It would be my last contact with any living being for the next month or so. I had grown to know Paul over the years, and we had familiar jokes between us about people on expeditions forgetting to pack crucial supplies. It's a feeling of unease that lingers at every departure.

"Did you remember matches?" Paul joked with a grin. "Sleeping bag?"

I smiled back at him. I had checked my packing multiple times. I was ready to go. I turned to face my path ahead. The afternoon air hung perfectly still between the peaks.

My expedition manager, Stevie Anna Plummer, would be watching my progress from Colorado, monitoring my movements through a SPOT satellite beacon and giving me weather updates through short satellite phone calls every day at 7:00 PM and, if needed, again at 7:00 AM. She would also be updating friends, family, sponsors, and anyone who was interested in my trip by posting notes on my blog, including occasional audio messages sent through the satellite phone.

My plan was to stop about an hour before it got dark, so I had to get moving. I started skiing in the vast field of snow stretched all around me, pulling the sled and dragging the pole.

As I made my way through the deep snow, I heard the plane sputter to life behind me. *BRUPPPPP!* Within minutes, it zipped by me on the ground, giant clouds of glistening snow billowing from its wings as it gained speed on the glacier. I watched as, finally airborne, the plane banked to the left and toward an opening in the jagged peaks. The Beaver's distinctive propeller cadence grew softer as I stopped to take in the scene.

Brrrrrrrum. Brrrrum. Brrum.

Then, silence.

With every solo trip I attempted on Denali, this moment always felt the quietest. I could feel the silence in my core. To me, it defined being alone. I could hear my heart thump. I could hear the *swoosh* of my lungs filling and releasing every breath. I could even hear the ticking of the tiny alarm clock I had tucked into a pack on my sled.

I turned to look around at the vast open glacier, then craned my neck to look up at the rocky peaks piercing the blue sky. The place felt grand and prehistoric, as if I were entering into an ice age. Once again, I belonged to the mountains, the only human cradled in the Alaska Range for miles on end. It was both comforting and upsetting.

Why in the hell am I here again? I wondered. Yes, Denali had shown me breathtaking beauty and idyllic serenity. But it had also delivered so much misery, loneliness, and failure. It had tried to kill me. Multiple times.

From base camp, I headed down Heartbreak Hill before veering right and ascending the lower Kahiltna Glacier, to the north. *Photo by John Walter Whittier*

Every time I had set out on Denali, I was reminded of words often attributed to Uemura: "In all the splendor of solitude . . . it is a test of myself."

I strode forward again on my skis. I hoped that, as in other years, the first day of the climb would be easy. The beginning of the route, which flows slightly downhill before beginning its gradual and then steep ascent, is a nice way to ease into the long journey. But this time it was a trudge. I marveled at how much conditions can change from year to year. The snow was far deeper and fluffier than I had ever seen it there. Just the tips of my skis poked through the unusually light and deep powder, and at times I was up to my thighs in fluffy snow. In other years, parts of the surface had been windblown as hard as concrete, allowing me to walk across it without leaving a track.

The deep snow obscured many of the crevasses more than usual, but it also formed stronger bridges over some of them, making them easier to cross. Where I couldn't see crevasses, I just had to hope the snow bridges were strong enough.

My sled pulled heavy as I plowed through, barely gliding. I looked back to find only the top of the bags strapped to the sled peeking through the surface of the powder. It felt even more difficult to pull than the 250-pound sled I had hauled to the North Pole a decade earlier. *Must be a sign of getting old,* I told myself.

With every couple of strides, I bent forward to punch a ski pole into the surface, trying to find hidden crevasses before they found me. *Go slow,* I reminded myself, adjusting to the pace of life outside of civilization. *There's no hurry. This is life again for the next month.*

I counted strides, twenty-five at a time.

One, two.

Punch.

Three, four.

Punch.

I had to rest after each count of fifty. At the count of one hundred, I slid a thin, four-foot bamboo wand from a sleeve buckled to my spruce pole and planted it about a foot deep in tamped-down snow. Those small poles could be my only guide to finding my way back safely if a storm came through. I hoped they wouldn't fall over. I figured each wand had about a third of a chance of surviving a storm. "Each one of those four-foot wands is my little friend out here," I explained later in my audio recorder, an easy way for me to journal during my trip. "I haven't gotten as far as naming them yet."

I stopped at about 4:30 that afternoon, giving myself just enough daylight to reorient myself into the routine of setting up camp. Climbing Denali in the winter meant going far slower—and setting up a lot more camps—than in the summer. I simply couldn't travel very far each day. I had only a few hours of daylight, I was carrying everything on my own, and I was breaking trail everywhere I went. Plus, the cold snow was more abrasive and difficult to move through.

I decided to camp not far from base camp the first night, at 6,750 feet. After the harrowing experience with the snow shelter on my previous attempt, this time I took an alternate approach to accommodations on the mountain. I had found what seemed like an ideal tent: a red geodesic, double-walled Hilleberg Soulo tent perfectly sized for one person plus gear, approximately seven feet by three and a half feet inside. It was made of super-strong, lightweight, silicon-impregnated fabric and could be set up simply with exterior poles that I could manipulate while keeping my fingers warm in gloves. I found a sheltered spot on the mountain and dug into the snow to make it level. Then I popped up the tent in minutes, tying it to skis and other items as anchors. I called it my Hilleberg Hotel.

After setting up camp, I heard the rumble of avalanches and icefalls from the mountains around me. It was an eerie sound the first few times I'd heard it, but I had grown less afraid of it by then. One year I had heard a low-scale groan below me in that spot, the deep cracks and booms of the ever-so-slowly-moving Kahiltna. I felt as if I were lying atop the belly of the glacial beast. In a way, I guess I was. But that day, in that place, I felt comfortable and safe.

Out of the corner of my eye, I saw a black speck move about fifty yards away. I peered at it and saw that I had a mountain friend: a raven. Ravens don't migrate and are known to hang out in spots on the globe that seem uninhabitable. Clever and bold, they are quick to follow climbers in Denali National Park in hopes of scrounging a meal.

I was happy to see the bird. Ever since circumnavigating Greenland, I've had a special reverence for ravens, which are honored in many northern indigenous cultures. At a low emotional point in my Greenland journey, in a vast area of fjords, I heard a squawk coming from a hill nearby. A raven was in distress with a piece of driftwood snagged on its leg. I approached the bird slowly, speaking to it in soothing tones, and eventually it trusted me enough to let me cradle it in my hand and gently remove the driftwood. I had helped the raven survive that day, and the raven had helped me, too, giving me strength and renewed energy to battle through the hardships of the expedition.

Seeing a raven on Denali, feeling the presence of another living thing while I was all alone, was a gift. I watched in awe as the bird's tiny body flitted around the frozen landscape. I had romantic notions of why it appeared to me that day, that it was looking for companionship in desolate surroundings just as I was. But I knew better. Deep down, I understood that he wanted food. I was okay with that kind of friendship, too.

I ate heartily that first night, reconstituting powdered mashed potatoes, dried peas, and precooked bacon. I had honed my menu over the years. In my early Denali attempts, I took about five thousand calories or two pounds of food per day—the same amount I had taken to the North Pole—but I found that I could eat only a pound and a quarter each day on the mountain. Darkness meant less energy spent during shorter workdays, and altitude weakened my appetite.

I left a few small globs of my dinner for the raven on top of the snow where the bird could find it, then I curled into my sleeping bag for the night. I set my alarm clock, clicked off my headlamp, and closed my eyes, replaying the route and my plan over and over in my head.

Chapter 10

Weaving through the Kahiltna

(6,700 feet to 9,400 feet)

As always on these winter trips, the alarm seemed to beep ridiculously early. It was pitch black outside, still hours before sunrise, as I wiped the sleep from my eyes.

Getting up early and creating a routine is key to success. It also became part of my mental survival. I marked my days by time, not by distance or accomplishment. If I set out every morning with a specific goal—say, traveling five miles—but got held back by poor conditions, an equipment snafu, or any other problem, I would end up disappointed and start to think negatively. The key to enduring long expeditions, I had learned, was to never let my mind wander too far down a path of negativity. Concentrating on the moment— or at least on something positive—sustained me.

So on Denali, instead of setting out to cover a specific distance every day, I woke up each morning at about 6:30 and got started on my long list of daily tasks: Scrape the frost off the inside of the tent walls and brush it off my sleeping bag. Prime and light my tiny stove. Grab the blocks of consolidated snow and ice that I had left outside my tent door the night before and melt them into water for the day. Drink as much as I could, sometimes hot chocolate or a homemade concoction of instant tea, Tang, cloves, and grapefruit powder. Eat breakfast. Stuff my sleeping bag into a compression sack. Dismantle the tent. Organize my sacks and tuck them into the blue duffel bag on my sled. Strap it all down with mountaineering cord.

It takes two to three hours to break camp. I typically forged ahead around 9:00 or 9:30 AM, just as daylight started to glow.

Still on the flat expanse of the Lower Kahiltna on my second day, I was traveling mostly cross-country. I started to develop a rhythm of movement over the vast glacial field. At times I used music on my iPod as a motivator, playing everything from classical pieces to Prince or Bob Dylan. Every now and then, I caught myself playing air guitar on my ski poles. Sometimes it was a comfort to hear a voice other than the one in my head.

The wavy surface of snow on a glacier can almost hypnotize a person; the subtle dips and ridges look like a distant pattern of ripples on a calm lake. That's all nice, but those are crevasses. I had to constantly remind myself not to relax, to remember that hitting a dip just the wrong way could mean death, either a quick end from falling and hitting hard ice or a long demise, stuck withering away inside a hole.

At about 4:30, as the sunlight faded, the view ahead stopped me in my tracks. The mountains around me had become silhouettes, just the highest peaks still aglow in fleeting rays of orange. The crescent moon cut a bright sliver into the sky as the horizon turned a beautiful shade of magenta, then dimmed to dark blue. Maybe it was the exhaustion after a full day of work. Maybe it was that spectacular view all to myself. Maybe it was the emotional music of Yann Tiersen's "Atlantique Nord" I had playing softly in my ears. Tears fell from my eyes. Moments like that filled me with gratitude and kept drawing me back.

I made camp for the night in peace and ease at about 7,500-feet elevation.

The deep snow continued to be a big obstacle the next day. It was so deep that when I took off my skis and stepped into it, I sank up to my crotch. When I got to 7,800 feet, I worried about how I would manage to pull my sled through such powder as I continued up the mountain. That section of Denali has been dubbed "Ski Hill." I would be skiing *up* slopes ranging from bunny hill to black diamond, with the bottom of my skis covered in climbing skins— lint-brush-like fabric with tiny, stiff hairs pointing down the hill. They would help keep me from sliding backward while still allowing me to glide forward smoothly.

As I plodded, my stomach rumbled with a strange craving for steak. I knew why. Four years earlier on that spot on the mountain, I had heard the distant hum of an airplane and watched it fly tighter and tighter circles around me. I didn't know what to make of it. As far as I knew, I was the only climber in the Alaska Range at that point, and I hadn't called for help. What was that plane doing? Just then, I saw a package fly out of the aircraft and land about a hundred yards in front of me. I feared it was an emergency message. Was a family member sick? I rushed toward the package, which was easy to find in the snow because it was marked with a peculiar purple splatter around it. I tore open the duct-taped paper bag and found it contained notes of well-wishes from friends, including a marriage proposal from someone I didn't know. Also, encased in bubble wrap, I found a still-warm steak sandwich and a small busted box of merlot wine. About a cup of the wine remained, and I stopped right there to eat and drink like a king for a night. More comforting than the food, the notes gave me an incredible feeling of reassurance that people were thinking about me, that I wasn't the only person on the planet.

Oh, man, a sandwich like that would taste good right now, I thought as I continued pulling the sled through the deep snow on my fourth attempt up the mountain alone.

With the sled's drag straining my back, I stopped and decided to rearrange a few things, moving about twenty pounds of gear from the sled to my backpack. Then I rolled the sled on its side to brush off any snow that might have been sticking on its underside, causing friction. I paused when I saw the bottom and shook my head, smiling. Before leaving Minnesota, I had put two layers of duct tape on the bottom of the sled to protect its smooth plastic from getting damaged during shipping, and the tape was still there. I had forgotten to remove it! No wonder that sled had been pulling so hard. I could only exhale with a hearty laugh, the only person in on the joke. *Oh well, count it as extra exercise,* I thought as I peeled off the tape.

As I started skiing again, I noticed the brand name on the side of my ski poles: One Way. Good thing I wasn't superstitious.

I woke up on December 21 to the distant sound of thundering avalanches, a sobering reminder of where I was. It was going to be my first rest day. Then I realized it was the darkest day of the year. I tried to put a happy spin on the situation by reminding myself that from then on, the sun would be a little higher and a little brighter each day.

The next day, I started a mountaineering practice known as "double-carrying." I left my camp and carried half my supplies, mostly heavy food and fuel, up to 8,700 feet, where I buried it all in a safe spot and marked it with wands. I then followed my tracks back down to camp for the night. The next morning, I would make breakfast, pack up everything else—tent, cook kit, sleeping pads, all the remaining food and fuel—and haul it up. By myself, it was simply too exhausting to carry everything at once as my buddies and I had done on our first trip and as I had tried to do on my first solo trip. This practice also helps with acclimatizing.

Double-carrying in some form is common on Denali and many other mountains. "Climb high, sleep low" is the mountaineer's mantra. I had read about it in climbing books and talked about it with Elías de Andrés Martos and Vern Tejas. On Denali, Ski Hill is a popular place to start double-carrying because the route steepens and the altitude there can affect a climber's health. On a solo trip, though, double-carrying meant traversing some dangerous terrain four times instead of two and separating myself from some supplies. But after three attempts, I felt it was the only way I could have a chance at summiting. I needed to take my time, acclimate, and preserve my energy. I kept three days' worth of food and fuel, as well as a camp stove and other necessities, in a pack strapped to my back in case I ran into an emergency or lost my sled down a crevasse or mountain slope.

I double-carried again on Christmas Eve day. Although it was a holiday, I was determined to put in a full day's work. But first I treated myself to a cup of coffee, the first I'd had in two months after deciding to give up caffeine during training. It was heavenly.

I hauled a cache to 9,400 feet, then returned to my tent at 8,700 feet and settled in to make the best of the holiday alone. I had wished my family and friends Merry Christmas on an audio message that I'd recorded the night before with my expedition manager, Stevie, hoping she would put it on my website where she regularly posted updates for people to follow my progress up the mountain. This would be the third time I was spending Christmas alone on Denali, and holidays always felt lonely. I missed cooking dinner for friends back in Grand Marais. I'd make chicken, buttercup squash, and garlic mashed potatoes for Christmas Eve dinner, and during the week, I would make French meat pies to give as New Year's gifts, a tradition I had started many years ago.

But on Denali, I had to make merry on my own. For Christmas Eve dinner, I made a special main dish: seafood ramen noodles. (Unfortunately, I couldn't seem to find the seafood in it.) I turned on a small transistor radio that I had bought for fourteen dollars at Buck's Radio Shack and tuned it in to Christmas music on a station out of Anchorage. The radio was extra weight and I couldn't use it often without many spare batteries, but hearing broadcasts helped me feel less isolated from the world.

I pulled a small pine sprig from my pack and gave it a good sniff. Ahhh. Fresh, green pine was a wonderful scent on a barren mountain, especially during the holidays. Stevie had started a tradition of sending pine with me a few years earlier, and I looked forward to smelling it ever since. I pulled the sprig through a small elastic loop in the ceiling of the tent: my Christmas tree. I tore a chocolate bar wrapper into the shape of a Santa Claus ornament, then folded a foil star from the wrapper of an energy bar. As I lay on my back in my sleeping bag, frost crystals fell from the tent's ceiling and onto my face with each snap of the wind. I laughed a little, thinking of my friend Mark Hansen. I could just imagine him looking at my situation and saying, "Some people just know how to party!"

As I drifted off to sleep, I allowed myself to think about home just a little. My son, Jacob, was a dad now, celebrating the holiday with his wife and two young daughters, my grandchildren. Where had the time gone? As Bob Dylan says in a song of my youth, I thought, *"The times, they are a-changin'."*

Christmas morning was not as festive. Still half asleep, I pulled the bottle I used to urinate in out of my sleeping bag. I thought I had screwed the lid on tightly. I hadn't. I spilled about a cup of pee

down my neck. Fuck! I sprang up, trying to flip any pee droplets out
of my sleeping bag and onto the floor of my tent, where they would
quickly freeze solid. I shook my head. It seemed like every trip had
some sort of nasty incident with bodily functions.

Merry Christmas to me.

The next day, I took half my load up to 10,200 feet, buried it in
the snow, and planted a long wand to mark it. I was near the top of
the Kahiltna Glacier, where the route ahead bent east. There would
be a good spot to camp at 11,200 feet, a sketchy traverse at around
13,000 feet known as "Windy Corner," and beyond that, the top
of Denali. I could see lenticular clouds streaming across the other

Working through deep snow on the upper Kahiltna, at about 9,500 feet,
I could see lenticular clouds in the distance, revealing strong winds near
Denali.

peaks, a sign that the wind was raging on Denali as well, and I shuddered, glad I wasn't there at that moment.

Traveling below Windy Corner was dangerous, and I was always a little nervous about that. I even remarked on it in my audio journal. "Really super-high winds can throw football-sized pieces of rock . . . off that peak at Windy Corner. I didn't believe it was true until I'd seen them lying all over the snow," I said. "All you need is a marble-sized one to hit you in the head . . . that'll put you out." But that was something I'd have to face later, so I tried not to think about it. At least skiing would be easier soon, I thought. The snow was firmer from the wind in higher elevations, and my skis would glide atop it. So far, it had been one of my more exhausting starts.

At about 2:45 PM, I turned to head back down to camp for the night at 9,400 feet. But first I paused to soak in another stunning view. Down the middle of the gently snaking Kahiltna Glacier in front of me, the sea of ice looked almost peaceful, like a plush and inviting blanket. Jagged mountains flanked its sides, and the sky glowed in lavender and red, the sun low on the horizon. It was one of those moments when I felt complete gratitude.

How does the sky turn that color? I wondered. *Is it dust or ice particles? Do the frigid temperatures make it so?*

It reminded me once again of the wonders of the planet. Every corner of the earth has something spectacular if a person takes the time to look at it and think about it.

There I stood, humbled by the spectacular scene. In an era of Facebook and Instagram, a person can find thousands of photographs of sunsets in Hawaii, but how many people get that view from Denali in winter?

Chapter 11

Storm Brewing

(9,400 to 11,200 feet)

I felt as if I had a coating of rust on all my joints the next morning, making them stiff and sore. It was an ibuprofen kind of day. It took me an extra-long time to pack up my camp at 9,400 feet. I couldn't get my sorry butt moving until after 9:45.

The route ahead would probably be arduous if previous experience held true. Strong winds are often funneled over the top of the Kahiltna, creating poor visibility from blowing snow. I hoped I could safely make it to 11,200 feet by the end of the day, where I could set up my tent cradled in a natural amphitheater—a roughly thousand-foot slope of rock to the north, an approximately eight-hundred-foot steep and snowy slope to the east, and tall icefalls rising to the south. The only narrow opening would be to the west. Climbers traditionally spend a couple of nights at 11,200 feet to acclimate, and I was looking forward to setting up camp there. I needed some rest.

The skiing was hard. Although the snow wasn't as deep and fluffy as it had been at lower elevations, the terrain was getting steeper. After about three long hours of skiing up, I was happy to finally spot the bamboo wands marking the cache that I had deposited the previous day at 10,200 feet. I loaded my supplies onto my sled and decided I would just take everything with me the rest of the way, knowing I would be catching up on rest soon at 11,200 feet.

It was a nice idea. Before long, I could see that I wasn't going to make it to 11,200—not at my slow pace. The altitude was starting to affect me more. Less oxygen filled my lungs with each hard-earned breath. The glacier was steadily steep. Each of my strides was getting shorter. My skis sank about six inches into the snow, and it was getting more difficult to glide. The higher and colder it gets on the mountain, the more abrasive the snow becomes, creating more friction. I felt as if I were dragging myself and my hulking sled over sandpaper.

After a couple more hours and only four hundred more feet of elevation gain since picking up the cache, I stopped to rest and consider my options at 10,600 feet. By then, it was about 3:00, and my energy was depleting, but I still had a long way to go. The path ahead was steep, and Denali was notoriously fickle for visibility in that spot. The winds had been picking up, coming up the glacier from the south. I could see blue sky overhead and to the north and east, but major gusts kept trying to push me around. A low-pressure system was coming in, but the forecast I had heard from Stevie didn't seem dire. Should I just continue on?

I weighed the pros and cons. It didn't make sense to try to camp where I was, in a steep and precarious spot, when I knew there was a flat amphitheater about six hundred feet higher. If I continued to carry everything, I figured it would be well past dark by the time I got there. If I ditched most of the weight I was hauling by leaving it in a cache and came back to get it in the morning, I could hope to get up to camp around dusk. Plus, I reasoned, the movement down and back up the mountain would help me acclimatize. And really, it wouldn't cost me much time overall. I could ski down to the cache in about fifteen minutes the next morning.

Leaving a cache was the obvious choice. I pulled out my compact snow shovel with its telescoping handle and dug a hole to bury the heaviest parts of the load from my sled. I marked the spot with my big, trusty black spruce pole, something I'd be able to spot easily from a long way away. I took far less than half the weight with me. I wouldn't be going very far, so I carried just the bare necessities, thinking it would be easy to get the rest in the morning.

The wind coming up the glacier, which I estimated at forty miles per hour, knocked my sled over on its side, a bad sign. Maybe that change in the weather was going to be more significant than I had expected. I just hoped I wouldn't be delayed for too long.

Carrying less, I made good time, about two hours. There was still a bit of light in the sky when I arrived at 11,200. Snow swirled in the air, but I could see a sliver of moon above me, evidence that the flakes were riding the wind, not falling from clouds. After finding a good spot to camp, I dug a space for my tent to protect it from wind and popped it up by the beam of my trusty headlamp after 5:30 PM.

I grabbed some leftover food that I had stashed in a bag on my sled, that day's half-eaten lunch of bacon, chocolate, and dried rye bread, and half a dinner of powdered mashed potatoes and peas from the night before. It was the ninth day of my trip, and I had been ravenously hungry for a while, but my appetite had leveled off, and I hadn't eaten my entire rations. That night, my appetite stronger, I ate a meal of mac and cheese and set my kitchen stuff to the side of the tent. I didn't even look inside my backpack before stashing it and some other equipment neatly outside the tent.

Curled inside my sleeping bag, I listened to wind gusts rattle the tent walls, vacillating between occasional sharp snapping sounds and stillness. I guessed that occasional gusts might have reached fifty miles an hour, common on Denali. I figured there was some snow headed my way, but I wasn't hugely worried. I turned on my radio to catch the Alaska Public Radio station out of Anchorage. I felt a little closer to my Minnesota roots as Garrison Keillor's smooth voice delivered tales on *A Prairie Home Companion.*

The only thing that gave me pause as I settled in to sleep that night was remembering that a team of four Japanese climbers had lost their lives about a hundred yards from where I was camped. In the summer of 2012, five climbers had been roped together when a small avalanche rushed down the eight-hundred-foot slope that stood directly to my east and knocked the climbers off their feet. The rope held them all together, and four of the climbers were buried for eternity. The lone survivor fell an estimated thirty feet into a crevasse and, miraculously, managed to climb out. He staggered all the way to base camp to find help. Rescue teams searched for the others but never found them. A lone wand still marked the spot.

Their bodies remained along with thirty-nine other corpses that had never been removed from Denali at that point. Unlike Mount Everest, where some bodies have been left in the open for other climbers to see, Denali's victims are out of sight. The National Park Service tries to recover all of Denali's fallen climbers, even those who are buried, but sometimes it's too dangerous or the climbers' bodies can't be found.

As I lay in my sleeping bag, I thought about how Vern Tejas had sworn that he felt the presence of Naomi Uemura in his snow cave. I wondered if the spirits of the Japanese team were still trapped there on the mountain near me. Would I see their ghosts in my dreams? Would I feel a comforting presence, just as I had felt

Annie's on the Northwest Passage so long ago? When all our senses are heightened, do we discover that we're never truly alone?

Before falling asleep, I put in a set of earplugs to dampen the sound of the rattling tent walls and made myself think of something positive. I was snug and warm there, and I was safe. After retrieving my supplies in the morning, I could rest for a couple of days. I didn't even bother setting my alarm, knowing I could get up at my leisure. All I had to do the next day was ski down to grab my stuff, then haul it up. It would take only a couple of hours.

Oh man, does this feel good, I thought as I drifted off, unaware of the wind continuing to increase outside.

Chapter 12

Stuck

The tent walls rattled violently when I woke the next morning after nine. I zipped open the door to a sea of white. I couldn't even see the giant rock slope about one hundred yards to the north.

I got dressed and got out of the tent to assess the situation. A foot of snow covered the supplies that I had left outside. I was in a protected amphitheater so I wasn't feeling direct winds, but strong gusts had managed to whip up the snow. It swirled around me as in one of those snow globes people display at Christmas. Thin lines of flakes obscured not only the dark rock wall but also the icefall and the saddle leading up to Windy Corner. Really, all I could see was my tent next to me, which had been buried even more by the snow. I knew I wouldn't be getting my cache that day.

Traveling in whiteout conditions is like pulling a sheet over your head and trying to find something without falling into a crevasse or falling off the edge of a cliff. You can't see drop-offs or rocks until you're right on top of them. The only reference to direction is the way the wind pushes you.

I had sat through many whiteouts before, and I didn't expect this one would last long. I dug out the one day's ration of food I had left in the sled—a gallon-sized Ziploc plastic bag stuffed with snacks that would serve as a breakfast, a lunch, and a dinner—and set it to the side of my tent. It wasn't much, but I still had the emergency supply in my backpack. I started to organize my belongings, and when I finally got around to unzipping the backpack, my stomach sank.

What?

I dug deep into it.

No food. No fuel. Just some extra clothes, an emergency locating transmitter, and my phone.

How was that possible? I kept rooting around in the pack. Had I missed it somehow? It couldn't just disappear. I always carried three to five days' worth of food and fuel with me.

Then I remembered. A couple of evenings earlier, I had rearranged some of my supplies. I often redistributed weight between my sled and backpack depending on the depth of the snow and the incline of the mountain. In steep spots, I wanted more weight on my back for traction, but on flatter terrain, I wanted more weight in the sled. Then I would normally take stock of everything at camp, making sure I knew what to double-carry and what to keep with me at various points. It wasn't always a perfect science. But had I really forgotten to restash the emergency rations in my backpack?

I went back outside to the sled and went through everything. I found nothing there either. Back in the tent, I spread out all my food to take stock. After everything I'd eaten the night before, I had about one day's worth of food left: a couple of chocolate bars, two energy bars, some bacon, a rice pudding breakfast, a partially eaten dinner, a pack and a half of Clif Blok energy chews that I had planned to use for the summit climb, some homemade sesame seed butter, and honey bars. I shook my fuel canister and guessed I had about two and a half days' worth of fuel left.

Calm down, I told myself. *Don't get your underwear in a knot.* There was a pretty good chance the winds were going to quiet soon, and I would be able to go get the rest of my supplies. If not that day, surely the next day. All I needed was a short window of decent weather. If I could just hike a little way around the corner, I knew I would be able to see my spruce pole. It wasn't that far.

I settled in for a storm day, passing the time by sleeping, completing small tasks, and trying not to worry. Between naps, I duct-taped tiny holes that had appeared on some of my jackets. I taped together a couple of bamboo wands to make larger markers for the cache I planned to leave at that camp so I could find it on my descent. I refined my game plan for what I would carry as I moved higher up the mountain. I switched out two layers of socks on my feet. While my boots were off, I used a spoon to scrape the ice that had accumulated inside them from my foot moisture. I pulled out the waffle-weave rubber insoles and popped out the tiny ice chunks that had formed in them, like ice cubes in a tray.

The tent shook violently in the wind. I worried it might get damaged, but I thought I had it shored up well enough. Every now and then, I would stick my head out the tent door to see what was happening outside. The air temperature felt balmy; I estimated twenty degrees. But the visibility was still horrible.

I ate only a couple of bites at each meal the rest of the day, trying to conserve.

All the while, Denali seemed to tease me. For short periods, I could see the rock slope, but ten minutes later, blowing snow would sock me in again.

I turned on the radio, and at one point a news segment mentioned a Minnesota man and his quest to successfully climb Denali
solo in the dead of winter. "I know that poor sap!" I said aloud.

I talked briefly with Stevie over the satellite phone at about
7:00 PM, trying to get a fix on the weather and my situation. As the
evening wore on and the winds grew stronger, I was reluctant to
open the tent door, trying to keep snow from flying in and melting. But I had to go outside at times to scrape the snow from the
tent walls and keep the storm from consuming me. All bundled up,
I tried to dart out as quickly as possible, rushing to zip the door
shut behind me.

Later that evening, the wind whistled and snapped my tent fabric
so much that I decided I needed to better protect my little haven. I
got up, pulled on ice-cold clothes over my long underwear, and
went outside to sink the tent further into the snow.

With the storm continuing to rage around me at 11,200 feet, I tightened
the guylines and sunk my tent deeper in the snow as protection from
the wind.

I had secured the tent by attaching it to equipment or stuff sacks filled with snow, then burying them, a technique called a deadman anchor. I unfastened a few of the anchors at a time, digging under the tent, then refastening as I went. The cold wind drove snow into my face, my cuffs, and the creases of my neck. Sinking the tent created walls of snow around it. I wondered how long I would need those walls.

Chapter 13

Still Stuck

I woke up in the middle of the night and started to worry about my food and fuel. And with all that wind whipping, I worried that the spruce pole marking my cache might have blown over. How would I find my stash then?

"Then I'm in some pretty serious problems," I said in a 3:00 AM audio recording. "I mean, normally you wouldn't stress about that stuff, but when your life depends on it, it's a different story. Ha-ha."

Later that morning, I came to the realization that I might be stuck for a long time. The wind was blowing, and the temperature was rising. A weather system was coming in. It was freakish weather. I had heard that Anchorage was forecasting rain. There were also high winds reported in the mountains. The weather reports from Stevie didn't sound good either. I knew it was all coming my way in a matter of hours.

Getting out of the tent to clear the snow away from its dome became a routine, as did digging out my gear to make sure I could find it in the fresh snowfall. I also used that time to answer nature's call.

The park service gives climbers compostable bags along with Clean Mountain Cans, practically indestructible nine-inch round, eleven-inch tall containers that seal up tight and are strong enough for climbers to sit upon, albeit awkwardly. Starting in 2007, the park service required climbers to remove their waste on the mountain's higher elevations because popular camps had become contaminated. Climbers are allowed to pitch poop bags into crevasses below 14,200 feet, though the park service encourages that human waste be packed out. Researchers are still studying what happens to the bags as they move slowly with the shifting ice, expecting they will eventually reach the glacier's ablation zone and melt out. Finding some contorted yoga position in which to use the can outside during a blizzard isn't pleasant. There's certainly no time to dilly-dally. But thankfully I never found the need to do that job inside the tent.

When I came back in, I decided to make a plan in case the storm lingered. "There's a bit of a dilemma unfolding here, and it's not good," I said into the audio recorder.

I laid out all my food on my ground pad and divided it up. *Storms are typically three to five days long,* I told myself as I parceled my rations into three piles, trying to stay optimistic. The three piles were pathetically small. Just looking at them made me hungry. *Fuck! I could eat all this right now and not be entirely full,* I thought. *How am I going to stretch this out?*

But starving wasn't my main concern. I worried more about dehydration and hypothermia. Operating outside in dry, cold air sucks the water right out of a person. And a body without calories won't stay warm, just like a woodstove without firewood. Warm sleeping bags and good clothes help, but even they won't keep you warm if your body doesn't generate enough heat inside them. The only way to generate heat is to have something to eat or drink that has calories in it. I would have to eat just enough to warm my sleeping bag system, piled with clothes on top, not knowing how long I would have to survive that way.

"The tragedy is . . . I could die right here in the tent with my food six hundred feet away, which is a very real possibility," I said into the recorder. "Pretty stupid move. I knew there was some bad weather coming in. I just didn't think it would sock me in for this long."

I got strict with my rationing, eating only a few bites at each meal and drinking only a few gulps. In between, I tried not to acknowledge my hunger. *Mmmmm. Mmmm,* I thought. *That tasted good. Now what do I do with the other twenty-three and a half hours in this day?*

Between more long naps, I tried to busy myself with small tasks. When I need to burn time, I'm a professional putzer. I can conjure up all kinds of silly stuff to do.

I dug out my tiny sewing kit and looked around. *What can I repair?*

I sewed a couple of stitches on my hood to make it a bit tighter. That took ten minutes.

I found a piece of parachute cord and made a better clothesline than the one I already had strung up in my tent to hang up wet clothes. That also took about ten minutes.

I scraped grime off my cooking pot.

I gave my teeth an extra flossing.

I tied a string around my spoon to attach it to the handle on my mug so I wouldn't lose it.

I used a piece of duct tape to attach a BIC lighter to a string around my neck so I'd always have a stove starter nearby.

When you're desperate, you look for the detail in everything. I imagine anybody who's been incarcerated has developed similar tricks. You just have to accept that what you're doing isn't really going to matter in the grand scheme of things. Concentrating on the minutiae is important simply to get through the day.

I updated my written journal, a small green wire-bound notebook. "Running out of things to do," I wrote. "There's a lot to do once I get my supplies from down low."

I keep journals on all of my expeditions, some in writing and some recorded on audio. It's a nice way to reflect on the day and pass the time. I like to keep a record in case I want to write about my experience later. After standing out in the elements without paper or pen, I learned to take an audio recorder with me. Too many times, I had thought, *I'll have to write that down later*, only to forget it. Plus, in subzero temperatures, it's easier to speak into a hands-free recorder tucked inside my clothing than try to scribble in a notebook.

I recorded my journal on the same iPod I used to listen to music and books on tape. I shuffled through my iPod's contents, hoping there might be some music in there I hadn't listened to. I was disappointed to find nothing new.

Okay, I told myself, *I'm going to get out of the tent and walk around to see if there's any improvement.*

It didn't look good. Maybe I could try walking a little, just march in the direction of my cache and turn around as soon as I thought I might lose sight of the tent. I set out, trudging due west, one boot in front of the other. I constantly glanced back at the red dome of my tent behind me. I got maybe twenty yards before it disappeared into white and I had to turn around.

Back inside, tucked into my sleeping bag system, I started to mentally beat myself up. How could I have been so careless? It would be stupid for me to die so close to my supplies. All of this could have been easily avoided.

I thought about all the mountaineers who had died in accidents because of one small misstep: misreading a cornice, stepping into a crevasse at camp, mistakenly getting separated from supplies. It's the simple routine that can kill us. Here I was, proving that true. After all the long and difficult expeditions I'd been through in my life, how could I get stranded six hundred feet away from my food and fuel? Could it really end this way?

Chapter 14

Atrophy in the Tent

I woke earlier than usual, less tired after two full days of doing almost nothing.

"The tent was completely covered under snow," I wrote in my journal. "Heard on the radio it's 34 degrees in Talkeetna. Weather's fucked. Here, it should be minus 40 or colder."

The more time that passed, the harder I had to work to manage my psyche. I was growing restless, but I tried not to get out of my sleeping bag unless absolutely necessary. Staying put would preserve my body's energy, extending the benefits of my measly food and water.

Being inside a tight sleeping bag system for so long can feel like torture. Most nights on Denali, I slept tucked into a vapor barrier liner, basically a nylon sack with reflective Mylar inside. It was completely waterproof and somewhat like sleeping in a plastic bag. Outside of that was a light winter-weight down sleeping bag. Outside of that was another light winter-weight synthetic bag, which handles moisture condensation better than down. I put all of this on top of two sleeping mats on the tent floor, one with large egg-carton-like bumps to trap air for extra warmth and to collect moisture.

In extreme cold, the sleeping bags were ice cold when I got into them to go to bed, so I would spend about forty-five minutes kicking and screaming, wrestling with myself, rubbing my core, trying to generate friction to heat them up. Once warmed, I often curled up in the fetal position, the bags cinched around my face. On the coldest days, only my eyes, nose, and mouth were exposed to the air, with my head and neck also covered in hats and gaiters. On warmer days, I had to be careful not to sweat and get my long underwear and the inside of my bag wet, so I would open the sleeping bag a little to let out some heat.

Typically, I kept candy bars nearby, so if I got chilled, I would have some calories to nibble on. In between sleeping bags, I kept a pee bottle and a water bottle so that both were easily accessible—always making sure not to confuse the two! I also kept a pair of synthetic booties inside my bag, extra insulation that I could pull on if my feet got cold.

Stuck in the storm, I lay in my bags in half-sleep, half-meditation mode. I started missing home. I longed to be with my friends in Minnesota, many of whom were taking vacations during the holiday week. I imagined them cozily celebrating by warm fireplaces, drinking wine, and laughing together. Whenever I started thinking about that, I tried to put my mind on something else. I invented a problem that I needed to solve or a plan I needed to create.

I sketched log cabins in my mind, trying to come up with structurally sound, energy-efficient designs that looked rustic as well as contemporary. I planned how I would build them while taking into account moisture management, insulation, roofing, lumber, and fasteners. I got as detailed in my thinking as I could, methodically planning every piece of construction in my head. It would bore the hell out of any right-minded human being, but it was a way for me to concentrate on something other than my predicament.

When I grew tired of making those plans, I looked around and tried to find something else to think about. I noticed details about how the tent material was stitched, with heavier threads weaved in squares among finer threads. At one point, I counted the number of tiny squares in about an inch of the nylon fabric. Trying to conjure the happy aspects of my adventures, I dreamed up plans for other expeditions I could launch after Denali. I decided on extended canoe trips in Canada and maybe going back to Greenland.

As the day wore on, still stuck inside that tent with little food or water, the biggest struggle became staving off my fears.

Chapter 15

End Is Near

For me, 2014 would go out with fury. On New Year's Eve day, the storm continued to rage, snow blowing sideways.

My record for time spent in a sleeping bag had been sixteen hours, set on a previous expedition. Now I had been in my bag for nineteen shivering hours. The pressure points on my body grew sore. I found myself turning like a rotisserie chicken: flipping from one aching shoulder to the other, lying on my back, then my front. It was getting increasingly difficult to find a comfortable position. My limbs grew stiff, my ribs were sore, and my muscles felt weak. Perhaps decades of construction work exertion were coming back to haunt me. I took aspirin and ibuprofen, both for pain and to help thin my blood to make it easier for my heart to pump.

Eventually, the aches and chills got so bad that I had to get up. I needed to get moving. After finally summoning the strength to slide into my cold clothes, I headed outside to brush snow off the tent.

"The snow is blowing so hard when I'm uncovering the tent that it nearly suffocates me," I wrote in my journal. "The fine particles seem to get in my nose and mouth, ears. . . . Between December 30 and 31, the tent has been completely buried five times already." It was still relatively warm, and I constantly worried that any bit of snow that made its way into the tent, riding on the wind or sticking to my clothes, would make everything even wetter. The humidity was making it more difficult to stay warm.

Back inside, I heard what sounded like tiny rocks hitting the tent's dome. What could that be? I poked my head outside and saw that it was sleeting.

Not snowing. Sleeting.

How was that possible? I was at 11,200-feet elevation on December 31, not far from the Arctic Circle. It should have been minus fifty degrees. But instead, I heard on the radio, a robin had been spotted at a bird feeder in Bethel, Alaska, earlier that month. It was nuts. The weather was turning into a freak show.

The walls of my tent dripped all over my down clothing and sleeping bag. I pushed them outside to rub in whatever dry snow I could find just under the surface, hoping the snow would suck out the moisture from the down.

Meanwhile, my stomach contorted with the dull, annoying, persistent ache of hunger cramps. My gut felt as if it were rolled up in a tight, empty knot. That night around dinnertime, I reached for a piece of the most substantial food I had left: bacon. Oh, how I loved bacon on the mountain. I called it a "mouthful of ecstasy." Dipped in caramelized maple syrup and vacuum packed, it was my favorite food staple. I had been saving it because it carried the most calories among the meager supplies I had with me. I figured it could sustain me through the night, and if the weather showed any sign of promise in the morning, I could get up with a fighting chance to find my supplies.

I rolled up a single strip and popped the whole thing in my mouth. Why torture myself with a bunch of tiny bites? I let it sit on my tongue for a moment to take in its full flavor. It was incredible. I could taste its smokiness as well as the sweetness from the maple syrup. *Man,* I thought, *bacon is the best food on the planet.* I used all my willpower to save one other piece of bacon and some Clif Bloks for the morning.

"My vacation plans have extended to Australia and South America," I wrote in my journal, trying to keep some humor. "Happy New Year."

I still hadn't told Stevie exactly how dire my situation was. I didn't want her or anyone else back home to worry unless things got truly bad. But at some point the danger becomes imminent, and it was nearing that point. So I let her know that I was running dangerously low on calories and fuel.

"Don't worry, Lonnie. Things always seem to work out," she told me.

Half laughing, I thought, *Maybe this is the time they don't.*

That night, huddled in my sleeping bags, I started to face the sobering reality of my predicament. Stuck in my tiny spot on the giant mountain for the fifth night in a row, I knew I could easily wither away there if the storm didn't let up. I had only a little bit of water left in my thermos. I shook my fuel canister and heard only a faint whisper of liquid. If I was lucky, I guessed, I could melt one more cup of water . . . maybe two. That could probably get me through the next day, but I wasn't sure I would have enough energy to make it through the next night. It takes weeks for a healthy human to starve to death and at least a couple of days to die of dehydration. But I was running out of calories, and the grim reaper of hypothermia threatened me.

A rescue was out of the question. Although I had taken out rescue insurance, nobody could reach me in this raging storm. No helicopter pilot could find me to drop supplies. No airplane could land there on steep terrain. If I couldn't even see six hundred feet below me, where my cache of food taunted me, how could rescuers ever find me? Besides, I would never want to put others at risk. If it came to it, searchers would have to look for my body after it was too late. I imagined them finding my supplies buried next to my spruce pole in the snow, my lifesaving cache untouched. There would be nobody or nothing to blame but me. I had made the crucial blunder of leaving too much of my food and fuel behind. I was responsible for my mistake, and I wouldn't want anybody to point to anything else.

On my audio message for the website that day, I tried to sound upbeat. "We have a clearing coming tomorrow hopefully, and I'll be able to start getting my stuff from down low . . . and then I start setting up camps up above," I said. "So anyways, Happy New Year, everybody! Buh-bye." Despite the optimism of my message, I was worried. I couldn't help but think about the worst that could happen.

I had plenty of power left in my satellite phone, enough to call my loved ones for important conversations. If the storm continued the next day, I decided, I would use it. I would take the opportunity to tell people good-bye, to tell them that I loved them. It was awful to think about. Who would I call first? What would I say? I wanted to convey something meaningful and memorable, parting words that would comfort them forever. How does a person do that? I thought about trying to put people at ease by making light of my predicament and saying something cheerful: "I'm gonna go on a pretty long adventure!" No, that was the wrong approach.

I felt sick that I wouldn't be able to talk to everybody, that my phone battery would run out eventually, and then I would be completely, utterly alone. It was crushing to think about how everything

that had led up to that point—all my friendships and family relationships—might soon come to an end.

Tears streamed down my cheeks. Life on this amazing and beautiful earth was such a privilege. It was unbearable to think about
what I would miss. I had so much more I wanted to do. Still, I'd
had a fantastic life, and I was incredibly grateful. Yes, I had regrets,
but I also had had the ability and the courage to live my wildest
dreams. How many people get to do that?

Too weak to waste energy by using pencil and paper, I made a
mental list: I'd contact Stevie first for our usual 7:00 PM call and
explain it all. Then I'd start making the tough calls to my closest
friends and family members.

I would call my mom, I would call my dad, and I would thank
them. "This is what I've chosen for my life. I've had a great life, and
I want to thank you for that," I'd tell them. "Do not mourn. Try to
celebrate what I've done."

I would call Jacob and ask him to forgive me for not spending
more time with him. I had missed large parts of his growing up,
but he had turned into a man who made me proud, and I would tell
him that. I had hoped that my expeditions could become an inspiration to him on some level. I had tried to live by example, and I
knew that I wasn't the epitome of a good father. It hadn't been my
main focus in life, and I was sorry for that. It was my biggest regret.
I would reiterate what I had always told him: "Make your own road;
don't take other people's roads. You're an individual."

I would call Kelly and thank her for being there for me during all
the years of our marriage.

I would remind my family to check with my attorney friend about
my will. I didn't have much to leave anyone except a couple small
rental cabins I had built, plus a few possessions. I tried to think of
who would benefit the most from getting certain items.

I would give Musa, my friend who worked with me on cabins each summer, the kilt I wore to work during hot days—something he cringed at with disgust. He would always say, "When you die, I want that narwhal horn you got as a gift in Greenland." I would give it to him.

I dreaded the thought of hearing their voices for the last time and of each conversation ending. No matter how much I prepared, I knew I could never say everything that I should. How can a person find the right words at a time like that?

I wondered how my loved ones would remember me. I wasn't worried about a public legacy. The average Joe doesn't remember who climbed a specific mountain or crossed a geographic pole. But I hoped that I had touched some lives with my expeditions. I hoped that people who were interested could learn from a few of the things I had done.

After thinking it all through, I made myself stop. I needed to conserve my energy, physical and mental. I told myself I would deal with everything in the morning. I pulled on a neck gaiter, put in my earplugs, clicked off my headlamp, and cinched my sleeping bag tight around my face. *There's going to be plenty of time for bawling tomorrow,* I thought, *plenty of time to worry about things then.*

Before sleep came, I gave myself a short pep talk. *How long could that storm really last? It has to start petering out.* Maybe the weather would clear enough for me to get my cache.

I needed energy to get up again. I couldn't stay up all night worrying. I rolled onto my side and went to sleep.

Chapter 16

Happy New Year!

I woke up in the middle of the night to biting cold and less tent-flapping—a clear change in the weather. It gave me hope.

At about 1:30 AM, I peeked outside my tent and, in the moonlight, saw the rocks and ridge just to my north. Oh, what a beautiful sight that was. "Yes!" I whooped.

But then I made myself calm down. All of that could change by morning. Would it stay clear enough for me to make a run for my cache? I would have to endure several more hours in my sleeping bag first, few calories left to burn in my body and now in colder temperatures.

Later that morning, I didn't even look out of the tent to see if it was travelable. I just suited up to go. There was no choice that late in the game. If I was going to save myself, it was now or never. I got up and pulled on my ice-cold clothes, bundling up in extra layers.

Outside the tent, the air was calm but looked hazy. Visibility on the ground wasn't great. Under any other circumstance, I would have waited in the tent for it to clear. But at about 9:45 AM, I dug my skis out of the snow, strapped them on, and set out down the hill into the hazy white air.

With each step forward, I was farther from the sight and security of the tent. I kept straining my eyes to see, but I could make out only what was directly in front of me. Traveling partially blind among crevasses and cliffs is incredibly scary, but with my life on the line, I had to try. Thankfully, after so many years on the mountain, I knew the stretch ahead as well as any, and I was thankful the terrain was somewhat familiar to me. I could travel partly from memory.

I glided slowly but steadily, stopping frequently to look ahead, squinting to find my black spruce pole through blowing snow. Every now and then, for a few seconds, I could see better. Then the wind would churn up again, biting my face and slapping my optimism.

Soon a large crevasse startled me, gaping directly in front of my skis, and I scrambled to stop my glide. I paused to catch my breath and slow my heartbeat. I turned to look behind me and realized there were crevasses there, too. I was surrounded. I had somehow threaded my way through a maze of crevasses without seeing them. I thought I had been traveling safely in the middle of a valley, where snow bridges are strong and crevasses are deeply buried. The dangerous crevasse field should have been on an embankment far to my left. But there I was in the middle of it.

Holy shit, I thought. *This is exactly why you never travel in these sorts of conditions.*

I had been incredibly lucky not to fall into a crevasse. I had been probing the snow a little bit as I went, but I realized that I had been skiing lengthwise, parallel to the crevasses, and had miraculously skirted between them. But now, standing in the middle of them all, the prospect of falling into one almost paralyzed me. I was far away from the safety of my tent and needed to find my way out of the mess I'd gotten into.

I took what I thought was the safest bet: turning directly on a dime with my skis and following my tracks back. As I retraced my path, I could see that I had crossed at least three massive crevasses. It gave me shivers. It was terrifying to look down into a large, icy hole that fades from light blue at the top into a cauldron of black.

As shook up as I was, I finally figured out where I was in relation to my cache, which brought some small relief. When I felt I had traveled far enough out of the crevasse field and was back on safer terrain, I pointed my skis more to the right, into the belly of that narrow valley. I looked for that pole again, but I wasn't seeing it. With a sense of dread, I kept wondering, *Did it blow over? Did it break?*

Finally I thought I spotted something: a tiny black vertical mark that stuck out from its stark white surroundings. "There it is!" I yelled to the mountains, brimming with joy and relief. I looked down for a second to adjust my ski, and when I looked back up, the black mark was gone, obscured once again by the blowing snow. Had it been a mirage? I had been wanting to see that pole for so long, I wondered if I was imagining things.

Moving on hope and adrenaline, I headed carefully in the direction where I thought I had seen the mark, scanning the white air in front of me every few seconds, but I couldn't see anything. That pole was a lifesaving beacon, and I absolutely needed to find it. I really had no sense of how far away it might be. I remembered how once on an Arctic expedition, we had thought we were approaching a small mountain, but after we went ten feet, we realized we had been looking at a dog turd. Seriously. Whiteouts can mess with a person that much.

After each stride, I turned my neck to scan widely in front of me. Finally, I spotted it again. This time I could tell; it definitely was the spruce pole. My big, beautiful marker. Just down the hill past the pole, everything was misted in. The only clear spot was between the pole and where I was standing. I breathed a deep sigh of relief and then sobbed for a few seconds. I would get to live. I would get to see another day.

"Shit, this has been hard," I said into my audio recorder. "Boy, what a lesson. It's a lesson I wouldn't want to put on anybody because it was really painful."

I knew how lucky I was.

"I've been graced," I said. "My stupidity has been graced with living."

Worried I might lose sight of that spruce again, I tried to triangulate it with a rock on a ridge above it and some ice I could see across from that rock. Then I kept my eyes trained on that pole as I raced toward it. I finally reached it at about 10:30 AM. I pulled out my shovel and dug through the deep snow at the pole's base, then scooped away snow with my arms until I scratched the top of the big blue duffel bag.

I was almost numb emotionally, so exhausted from the stress and worry. Now I could finally relax. For the first time in days, I didn't have to think about the scenarios from not finding that bag. I slid open the zipper and beheld the smorgasbord in front of me. I gulped the first high-calorie item I could reach: chocolate. Then I poured some powdered goat milk and sugar into the remaining bit of water in my thermos and shook it up, knowing I needed easy-to-absorb calories and nutrients along with hydration. I wanted to devour everything, but I forced myself to eat slowly. I couldn't afford to get sick by putting too much in my cramped stomach too quickly.

I packed up the sled and started back for my tent. The sled was full and heavy, and I was weak from the storm, but I barely felt it.

My adrenaline was in gear. The air had cleared a little, and I knew my path back up to camp contained no crevasses. I was so elated to be moving with a little food in my stomach after being confined for so long. I stopped to eat morsels of a Ritter Sport bar with chocolate, hazelnuts, and raisins, savoring the sugar and caffeine it was feeding my body. It tasted so good, it was almost sinful.

The trip back up to camp was arduous. I had to stop and rest every few yards, my body drained of energy as I tried to pull a heavy load again. When I finally got back to my tent at about 1:30 PM, my weakened body felt numb and stiff. Any movement was an effort, but my brain was racing. I melted snow to make water and consumed small amounts of food and drink all day: energy bars, chocolates, pieces of bacon.

Most people would call it quits after an ordeal like that, I figured. They'd say they had learned their lesson and felt lucky to have survived. They would get the hell off that mountain. I could understand that, and I couldn't have been more grateful to be alive. I had learned my lesson to check my supplies. But that episode was over now. Should I give up?

I spent a couple of hours building a snow shelter. It gave me something to concentrate on, and if I decided to keep going, I would have an emergency shelter available on my way down.

That night, the thermometer outside read minus twenty-two degrees, but inside the tent, I lived a little in excess. With plenty of fuel after living on skimpy rations during the storm, my stove roared in my dimly lit hovel. My natural instinct was always to be stingy with fuel and use it only for melting snow into water, not for heating the tent. But now that I had extra fuel, I broke that tenet and warmed the air to well above freezing. I even dried out a few pieces of clothing. Ahhh, luxury.

I ate well, too: mashed potatoes, macaroni and cheese, more chocolate and bacon. I drank as much as I could to restore my fluids. Hot chocolate and hot Tang kept me warm inside. I was still hungry, but I was comfortable again.

I worried about the toll the whole ordeal had taken on my health. I was weak, but would I recover enough for the rest of the climb? Or would it be like my previous attempt two years earlier when I found myself spent just short of the summit?

I wrestled with the decision. Should I turn back?

Chapter 17

Forging Ahead

(carrying a cache to 12,300 feet)

One way or another, I wanted to get the heck out of that camp at 11,200 feet. Whether I went up or down, I had to leave.

I get most depressed when I'm not moving, not making progress. Being stuck in one place for so long makes me stir-crazy. Yes, I needed to regain my energy, but that would happen over time. The best thing I could do for myself, both mentally and physically, was to start moving.

I decided to climb up.

I planted a small cache of food and fuel at my 11,200 camp and stuck my skis vertically in the snow, a reflective wand taped to them. The rest of the mountain would be too steep to ski up. Instead, I strapped on my fourteen-point Black Diamond stainless-steel crampons. I hoisted my backpack onto my shoulders and tethered my sled and my spruce pole to my waist. I grabbed my ski poles to bring with me for added purchase and balance. I started pulling half my load—a triple-checked half this time—up the steep, crevasse-filled snow chute above 11,200 feet, overjoyed to be advancing past that place.

I moved agonizingly slowly at first on that steep stretch. The first obstacle on the path was the crevasse where the Japanese climbers had fallen to their deaths in the avalanche. I strained to stretch my leg over its narrower end and heaved myself across it while pushing on my ski poles. I avoided looking into the crevasse. Logically, I knew the climbers were long gone, deep in the recesses of the glacier, but I couldn't help but think that I might somehow catch a glimpse of them if I looked down.

The day's climb was excruciating. I was hoping to deposit my cache at about 12,900-feet elevation, but my progress slowed as the day went on. My backpack, my sled, my body: it all felt so, so heavy. My legs moved slower and slower, every stride a herculean effort. Three steps. Pause. Breathe. The burdensome load put extra pressure on my feet, making my toes cold. I had to remind myself to keep wiggling my toes inside my stiff mountaineering boots no matter how much it hurt. I longed for the soft moose-hide mukluks I wore on my polar expeditions.

Finally reaching a small flat section at 12,000 feet, I decided I had to do something about my numb feet. I leaned on my ski poles to take pressure off my soles and alternated swinging one leg and then the other, allowing warm blood to flow to my little piggies. During about fifteen minutes of this maneuver, the numbness turned to pain, then back to feeling as if I once again had toes.

I continued to lurch up, and when I made it to about 12,300-feet elevation, I had to call it quits. Every muscle felt tired, shaky, and weak, an aftereffect of lying around for days stuck in the storm.

I stood in a giant bathtub-like trough in the ice that had been carved out by high winds. I turned my sled upside down and pinned it to the surface with an ice screw. I set off my locator beacon so people knew that I was on the move again after so long in one spot. I may have been weak and dead-tired, but at least I was back to making progress, depositing a cache up the mountain.

On the way back down to 11,200 camp after depositing my cache, I fixated on how I would savor a bowl of mashed potatoes topped with a dollop of calorie-packed, savory duck fat; get a good night's rest; and see what the next day would bring.

Chapter 18

Getting around Windy Corner

(11,200 to 14,200 feet)

Some days, the mountain's messages were more cryptic than others.

After packing up my tent and supplies the next morning, I was feeling more positive about the rest of the journey. On a pitch of marble ice at 12,600 feet, I was reinvigorated when my friend the raven showed up, flying in front of me over a small plateau. The higher I climbed, the more comforting it was to see something alive. Knowing this black bird could fly so high, from so far, and in such cold, I somehow felt less isolated.

It was especially nice to see life in that spot, which was particularly foreboding. Scoured by the wind, the ice on the plateau's edge had been polished dark blue, almost black, but with rounded bumps. It was so smooth and hard that even a sharp crampon hardly left a scratch. The whole area was peppered with rocks, ranging from small as peas to large as footballs. They had fallen or blown hundreds of yards from Windy Corner just above. It was a dangerous place to spend time on a windy day.

Just after I watched the raven fly around me, I looked down to find a curious relic partially embedded in the ice in front of my boot: a two-inch-long ornate crucifix. Out of instinct, I bent down to pick it up. I looked it over, cradling it in the palm of my deer-skin mitten, then put it in my pocket. As I started climbing again, I wondered what it meant. What were the odds of my finding that on the vast West Buttress? Was the mountain trying to tell me something? A climber must have dropped it there over the summer, I figured. I wondered what had happened to him or her. Had this been an important part of someone's journey? Had it been lost on the way up or on the way down?

I walked about ten paces and reconsidered. This cross belonged to the mountain now, I thought. I set it down, hoping it wasn't giving me some type of warning.

A few hundred feet higher, I reached the notorious Windy Corner. There, between 12,800 feet and 13,500 feet, climbers have to keep catlike focus as they scamper almost horizontally across a slope of icy snow, balancing against the driving wind. Monster crevasses wait to catch them below . . . and below that, a 1,500-foot icefall.

I had a tumultuous history with Windy Corner. In prior years, gusts near fifty miles per hour had tried to knock me down, blowing my sled sideways and rolling it perpendicular to my right, tangling its lines behind me. One year I had to hit the deck, flattening to the ground on my stomach whenever a strong gust approached. I chopped my ice axe deep into the hard pan and dug in the toes of my crampons to keep the wind from getting a grip on me. I performed that stunt a half dozen times before making it around the corner. But this year, Denali seemed to be in a better mood. It was a picture-perfect day. Miraculously, the wind seemed to die down as I approached. It was probably the calmest crossing I had ever made.

Then, as I worked my way up to camp at a plateau at 14,200 feet, Denali delivered an almost supernatural, spiritual moment. I was concentrating extra hard on weaving around the monstrous crevasses just before the plateau, making my way forward in a big scalloplike pattern. This was the stretch where Buck had fallen through a snow bridge on our first trip, so I was always on high alert.

The sky was darkening, and I could make out the dark voids just outside the beam of my headlamp. I stopped at the lip of a giant one, which had an opening that looked to be thirty to thirty-five feet across. I realized my spruce pole wouldn't even touch the sides until I was about one hundred feet down into it. Clear of the crevasses and approaching the safety of the plateau, flat and white like a frozen Minnesota lake, I found that the world around me had fallen dark except for the stars. The universe sparkled down on me with a clarity I had rarely seen.

I trudged forward to look for a place to make camp when a bright light caught my eye. It was coming from a couple hundred yards away, from a large vertical crack in an icefall on Denali's south face. It looked like a spotlight beckoning crowds to the grand opening of a Broadway play. My brain immediately jumped to farfetched conclusions: Was it someone's camp lit by a lantern? But wait, it was January. Was I delusional? Obviously I was the only one up there at that time of year. Finding another human on the mountain in January would almost be like discovering life on Mars.

I moved toward the spotlight almost in a trance, staring intently at the light, trying to figure it out. As ridiculous as it seemed, I scanned the ambient light around it for people. As I stepped closer, the moon appeared around Denali's east face, and I suddenly realized what I was looking at: rays of moonlight were bouncing through crevasses at just the right angles, refracting into a single spotlight toward me. Incredible!

Within minutes, as the moon continued to move, the light slowly faded away. What a strange, wonderful phenomenon it had been. Moments like that make up for the suffering and the hardship on expeditions. Each trip seems to bring an unimaginable, inspiring surprise or two. Each journey reveals something new.

I was the only person in the entire world to see that spotlight, but at that moment, I longed to share it with someone else.

Chapter 19

Waiting to Commit

(14,200 to 16,300 Feet)

I zipped open my tent to spectacular sunrise views at my 14,200 camp the next morning. All around me, the mountains seemed to glow, even distant ones beyond the Alaska Range. It was incredible.

"All the peaks are just tipped with a bright orange-red color," I said in my audio journal. "I've never seen it that way before in all the trips that I've done up here."

It was hard to stay put on such an ideal morning, but I had adopted a strategy on this attempt to give myself more rest and better acclimatizing. I spent a rest day doing chores and plotting out my plan to reach the summit. On every previous attempt, I had gone straight from 14,200 to the high camp at 17,200 feet, but this time I would camp somewhere in between and double-carry supplies.

My body had been adjusting well to the height. Except for a mild headache, I had no signs of altitude sickness. All things considered, I was feeling pretty good. "Not too many aches and pains," I said in an audio recording. "Heh, heh, for my age, I guess."

Even my raven friend was still flying strong. I pitched him some duck fat and bacon, hoping that he would keep coming back.

My camp at the 14,200-foot plateau offered a spectacular view of Mount Hunter to the south.

The next morning, I set out to take half my supplies up to the top of the headwall, the nine-hundred-foot, forty-five- to fifty-five-degree pitch where the park service puts fixed ropes for climbers in the summer. In the winter, snow and high winds create mostly ice on the headwall, and it appears blue.

When I got to the headwall's base, above 15,000 feet, I saw no ropes. Sure enough, the pitch was buried in a wall of winter snow and ice. I could see the silhouette of ropes in spots, and if I wanted to use them, I was going to have to bust them free.

It made for a long and onerous ascent. I began climbing with a hammer axe in one hand and an adze in the other. I used my hammer to bust through the ice to free the fixed rope, but it was taut like a guitar string. I clipped a carabiner to it and tried to pull up on it to rip it from the wall of ice. It took all my strength to get just a few feet to pop through the surface. From then on, I reached with my hammer as far above me as I could to pound and fracture the ice to help break the rope free a few meters at a time, and I used an ascender to slowly make my way up the wall.

It was exhausting work ascending a steep slope at nearly 16,000 feet with a heavy pack that wanted to throw me off balance. The weight and the steep angle put pressure on my feet and toes, making them cold. Part of me thought it would be easier to free-climb the thousand feet without a rope at all rather than try to pull the fricking line through the ice. But I had to go back down and then climb it again with the rest of my stuff, and I didn't want to try free-climbing it multiple times.

Back at my 14,200 camp, I decided to move into a snow shelter the next day. I had extra time, so I made it roomy, complete with separate spaces for a kitchen, dining room, bedroom, bathroom, and storage shed. You can take the man out of construction, but you can't take construction out of the man, I guess.

As I sat in my cave organizing my stuff, I remembered that one of my scariest episodes had been in a snow shelter at that elevation in 2012. My headlamp had been flickering one night, so I pulled it off my head and flipped open the battery compartment to readjust the three AAAs inside, thinking one of them had become dislodged. When the compartment opened, the batteries sprung loose and spilled onto the floor.

The entire cave went pitch black. It was an incredibly isolating feeling. I froze for a minute, trying to figure out what to do. I felt around the hard-packed floor of the shelter trying to find the batteries among my belongings, but I had no luck. They must have slid somewhere. I had extra batteries in a pack somewhere, but I wasn't sure if that pack was inside or outside. Going out to try to find the

Although I brought a tent for shelter, I also built snow caves at my camps at 11,200 and 14,200 feet as a backup in case winds damaged the tent.

pack and the batteries in the dark would require getting bundled up, opening the shelter, and letting in a bunch of cold air. That wasn't a good plan either.

Calm down, I told myself. *If nothing else, I can just stay here in the dark until it gets light again. I'm not dying here. I'm just freaking out.*

I took a deep breath and decided to just think things through and solve the problem. I started considering other electronics that used AAA batteries and where they might be. I remembered my SPOT beacon, which I had somewhere inside with me. I rooted around the cave until I felt the beacon, then carefully opened the battery compartment, all by feel. I took out three batteries, then carefully felt the inside of the battery compartment of my head-lamp, trying to figure out which ways the batteries had to go in based on the tiny springs and metal flaps. I periodically tucked my hands inside my sleeping bag to warm them up again. The whole ordeal probably took an hour and a half.

I considered myself fortunate. If I'd had to wait until morning light peeked through my vent hole, I might not have had enough time to finish all my chores and get going for the day. I could have wasted an entire day of travel just because the stupid batteries had popped out of my headlamp at the wrong time.

Years later, it felt luxurious to have such space in a snow shelter as I stretched among my belongings, neatly placed in their "rooms." In the morning, I wouldn't have to take down and pack up my tent. I could get going extra early.

After a night of restful sleep, I woke up and got dressed, eager to attack the headwall again and push toward the summit. I was all ready to go with my harness and crampons on and my camp all packed away.

But when I looked out of my snow cave, I was greeted with a complete mess of a storm. Winds were battering the plateau at about forty miles per hour, I estimated. The wind chill had to be about minus thirty-five degrees. I stayed outside, walking back and forth for a while, trying to figure out what the hell to do. Climbing in wind stronger than twenty-five miles per hour is not smart, so there really was no choice. I was stuck again. I hoped it would be just a temporary blip in the weather.

At least I had plenty of food and fuel with me this time. I was ravenously hungry, even after devouring four servings of potatoes with peas for dinner my first night at my 14,200 camp and four servings of mac and cheese the next. Psychologically, I was going stir-crazy being stuck again.

The plateau at 14,200 is the spot on the mountain where the rubber meets the road in deciding whether to go for the summit. From there, I would lighten my load dramatically, schlepping only a carefully selected pack and wearing a down suit with a one-piece wind suit over it. I would leave my sled and ski poles behind. If I made it up to camp near 16,000 feet or to high camp at 17,200 feet and got caught in a long storm, I wouldn't have the food and fuel—or the drive—to try to summit anymore. Strained by altitude, there's basically no coming down and trying to go back up at that point. If something went wrong and I lost forward momentum, I would likely just abandon the mission and get off the mountain, unfulfilled once more.

I got weather reports from Stevie, who was watching the predictions from NOAA (the National Oceanic and Atmospheric Administration) and a website called Mountain Forecast. Even if the weather improved the next day, a low-pressure system was sitting in the Gulf of Alaska, waiting to sweep into the mountains at some point, and I knew the window of clear weather could close at any moment.

By that point, I had spent hours visualizing the route ahead. After the headwall, I would reach the West Buttress ridge, an exposed, windy section with only one or two spots to put up a small tent. The first half of the ridge requires wriggling between and around rocks. One rock, dubbed Washburn's Thumb, is roughly the size of a UPS truck standing on end. It blocks so much of the ridge that it requires climbers almost to make love to it in order to slither by. I thought I might camp before it at about 16,300 feet to break up the climb and acclimate, even though it would be a precarious place. From there, it's a delicate catwalk on an exposed narrow strip with approximately 2,000-foot drop-offs on each side, the Peterman's Glacier on one and the 14,200 camp on the other.

I would place high camp again at 17,200 feet—the large open spot where most climbers stay before attempting the summit—and hope for another twelve- to thirteen-hour window of clear weather to scramble to the top and get back to camp. I would cross a small plateau, then the steep Autobahn, climb to narrow and windy Denali Pass at 18,200 feet, then take a sharp right and follow the ridgeline past striped formations known as Zebra Rocks around 19,000 feet. Then I would cross a plateau known as the Football Field and start the steep climb up the summit ridge.

I would take off on summit day at about 4:00 AM in hopes of summiting by 2:00 PM so I could quickly turn around and get back down just at dark. With a low jet stream and surprise storms constantly consuming Denali, especially in winter, any time spent on the summit is borrowed time.

I had the summit attempt all planned out in my head, but there I was, stuck at 14,200 in bad weather for an extra day. I was uneasy, wondering how long the storm would last and whether I could handle another one.

"It's just a really a nerve-wracking day. Makes me want to cry," I said in my audio journal, exhausted and pessimistic. "I'm starting to figure out, well, should I just hightail it out of here the first chance I can get in order to keep myself from spending a week in a snow cave looking at the ceiling? Or do I hope the weather changes and improves, and I can go for a summit attempt?"

Denali was fickle. I was wrestling the mountain physically and emotionally unlike any other terrain in all my years of exploring. How long could I keep this up? Was a January solo climb simply asking too much from this North American behemoth? Or was I just being skittish?

I tried to sound more upbeat on my audio message for the website. "I wanted to talk a little bit about the psychological difficulties you have on a trip like this. It mainly is just the waiting for good weather so you can move, and there's nothing worse than having to stay put, especially when you've got eighteen hours of darkness every evening. It makes for very long nights. . . . And of course there are always worries about safety and supplies and those kinds of things. . . . I'm trying to stay positive."

Just as I wallowed in my frustration, a report from Stevie said the barometric pressure was rising, and the forecast showed a window of decent weather, with winds mellowing below twenty-five miles per hour. Filled with renewed optimism, I figured the best day for a summit attempt would be in three days: Sunday, January 11. Then I waited—and hoped Denali would finally allow me to pass.

"If this has taught me anything, it's taught me patience and how to be still," I said early that day, speaking into the recorder. "Because in life outside of this snow cave, I'm anything but still."

Chapter 20

Go for It

I woke up after midnight and saw the seams between the snow blocks of my cave's roof illuminated by the moon. Clear skies? I hoped so. Sometimes the seams could be illuminated even if it was overcast. A little bit of snow was still blowing into the cave, but I crossed my fingers that it was simply from the wind, no longer a storm.

Indeed, the weather appeared to be clearing above me in the morning, and I let out a huge sigh of relief. I felt good. I felt rested. The clouds eventually yielded to bright rays of sun.

As soon as I could see the weather was going to be good, I was out of there. All my stuff was already packed and ready to go. I left behind in the snow shelter everything I wouldn't need for the summit.

Standing at the base of the headwall, I looked up at the steep and icy obstacle before me. I had to take one deep breath for each roped step. But at least the ropes were clear after I'd chopped them out. The climbing was much easier the second time around. I was carrying just a backpack stuffed with my tent, sleeping bags, sleeping pads, a few electronics, a stove, a shovel, five days' worth of food, and six days' worth of fuel.

My friend the raven greeted me as I ascended, but he disappeared before I got to the top. Lucky for him because I might have tried to squeeze his little neck.

I had stashed a sack of food and supplies between large rocks at the top of the headwall, covering it with small rocks. When I reached the top to retrieve it, I found a red fuel canister sitting precariously at the edge of the wall. What the hell was that doing there?

I went over to my bag and saw that the raven had managed to poke through its thick nylon fabric, something no human could do without a sharp tool. The bird had pulled out some duck fat and a couple of meals as well as the fuel bottle. That little pig! I had been saving the duck fat for high elevations, where I would really need the energy, and the damn raven ate the whole tub. What betrayal! Fortunately, I had some extra food, and I knew I would probably be fine.

It was dark by the time I found the narrow and windy spot on the West Buttress ridge where I could set up my tent, around 16,300 feet. For one of my tent anchors, I used an ice axe, pushing the handle in right at the edge of the ridge overlooking 14,200 camp. *This is a little close,* I thought. But it was the flattest spot available up there. I told myself, *Just don't roll over the wrong way.*

I had a headache, likely from the elevation gain and dehydration. I blew my nose, and blood boogers came out. Cold, dry altitude will produce those.

I tried calling Stevie as normal, hoping for another weather update, but in paring down my supplies, I had brought only one of my two satellite phones with me. I had grabbed the one with fresh batteries, but for some reason it wouldn't dial out. For an hour, I tried to make it work. The phone showed that I had a decent signal, but I couldn't get my call to go through. I dialed and redialed, positioning the phone different ways and in slightly different spots

My camp at 16,300 feet on the West Buttress ridge

to see if I could get it to work. I grew concerned that friends and family back home would be worried about me if I lost contact. I read the instructions on the phone again, wondering if my mind was perhaps clouded from altitude. It just wasn't working, and I didn't understand why.

I thought about the people back home who had been following my trip, expecting regular updates. "They're going to be worried," I said into my audio journal. "I'm more worried about people just being worried about me than me being able to talk."

At least I had a SPOT beacon that I could set off with a simple message through a satellite to let people know I was okay. There was no way I could tell for sure if that was working. I hoped so.

My nervous energy building with anticipation, I woke up the next morning to tackle what I considered a tough part of the mountain: the West Buttress ridge leading to high camp at 17,200 feet.

The ridge is mostly rock with some patches of snow. It's not technically difficult, but getting through it is hard work. One section about fifty yards long is so knife-edged that in the wintertime, it's almost too narrow to walk. One year I used two axes, holding them high on their shafts and daggering the picks into hard-packed snow, crossing just below the ridge by moving my legs side to side laterally. Other years, I climbed the ridge in the dark, which in some ways was okay because I could see and concentrate only on what was illuminated in the circle of light from my headlamp. Had I been able to see the whole picture, I might have shit my pants and tried to turn tail on the spot. In 2015, it was just wide enough to walk on top, but there was no place to dig in my axe. It felt as if I were walking on the world's highest balance beam. I had to completely concentrate on my footing, at some points straddling the ridge, a crampon on each side.

At moments like that, I longed to be part of a roped team. If one member falls in an area such as that, the others can arrest his or her fall. Or if he or she can't stop the group's slide, the rope will likely catch on rocks, preventing a two-thousand-foot plummet to certain death. Solo, I felt extremely vulnerable. Something as simple as snagging a crampon on a pant leg could spell the end of me. This time I walked gingerly across the top, using my axe as a cane for balance.

I reached the plateau at 17,200 feet in the daylight for the first time on any of my solo trips. Because I was coming from 16,300 feet—not my camp at 14,200 feet as usual—I had more time to rest there, acclimate, hydrate, and prepare for the summit attempt. The small plateau itself isn't always pretty, raked over by gale winds revealing piss spots and debris from summer climbs. There are splintered bamboo wands, lost aluminum pickets, and one year even a shovel left behind.

But the view from there is astounding. Looking out, still three thousand feet from the top, I felt as if I were already towering above the Alaska Range. To the southwest, the peak of Mount Foraker glistened, topping out just a couple hundred feet higher than where I stood. Mount Hunter, at 14,573 feet and about eight miles to the south, appeared small. On each peak, the weather looked clear with no lenticular clouds. I hoped with all my heart that it would stay that way.

I had left the nonworking satellite phone at my 16,300 camp—why carry the weight?—and I was a little worried about not having that connection to the outside world. I had to remind myself there was nothing I could do about it. Some people might call the phone a lifeline, but it really just provides a false sense of security. At that point on the mountain, it wouldn't do much good for getting me out of a bad situation anyway. My main concern was that Stevie might call for a rescue if she didn't hear from me for forty-eight hours, which was part of our plan.

But I couldn't call Stevie even if I wanted to, so I didn't have to worry about checking my watch to dial at our appointed time. It was just me—no more weather reports from civilization. I was free of ties to the outside world. I would have to rely on my own instincts, intuition, and judgment.

My stomach tightened with the anticipation of summiting. Finally, the conditions were looking favorable. But the summit run—an exhausting day under any circumstances—would still be fraught with risk. I decided to cherish my time alone at the high camp, soaking up the beauty surrounding me as much as I could. I also forced myself to eat some seafood macaroni and cheese. Appetite fades at such high altitudes, and the thought of food almost made me ill. But I had to eat and drink as much as I could. Being fully fueled and hydrated before pushing for the top was essential.

I organized my gear, though there wasn't much to get ready. I would be carrying only one chocolate bar, one and a half packages of Honey Stinger energy chews, one ice axe, and an extra set of batteries for the headlamp I'd be wearing on my forehead. I had four liters of water in a hydration bladder under my down suit to keep it from freezing.

I set my alarm for 3:00 AM and tried to sleep that night, brimming with hope and anxiety. *Sleep!* I told myself. *I've already done plenty of thinking. It's time for rest.*

The hardest part of the entire expedition was awaiting me, if I was lucky.

Chapter 21

Seizing Summit Day

Deet deet deet. Deet deet deet.

The beeping of the alarm clock came in total darkness. It was 3:00 AM, but I bolted awake. The tent walls hung silently, a good sign. I got out of my sleeping bag, almost oblivious to the cold as I took a deep breath and unzipped my tent door to look outside.

Stars.

Game on! I thought.

I started the stove and melted chunks of snow and ice that I had dug out and set in the tent vestibule the night before. I poured the warm water into my hydration bladder along with a little bit of Tang powder. If it's good for astronauts, it's good for me.

I took care of my morning business outside, and then I dressed up. In addition to my two layers of long underwear and a pair of wind pants and a hoodie, I pulled on my one-piece down expedition suit and, over that, a one-piece wind-stopping shell with a wolverine ruff, its long guard hairs designed to deflect biting winds from my face. I carefully pulled on a pair of thin wool socks, making sure there were no creases in them to irritate my skin. Vapor liners went over those and then a medium wool sock and a heavy wool sock.

I slid my feet into my boots with their custom liners inside and laced them securely. On my hands, I wore thin wool liner gloves, knitted wool mittens with the lanolin left in, and large wolverine fur mittens with smoke-tanned deerskin palms. I pulled on a neck gaiter that could cover my face up to my eyes if I needed it to. I wore a knit hat and cinched my hoods. In addition to my headlamp, I carried goggles in case of a storm, my SPOT beacon, and my GoPro camera.

I zipped up the tent and started walking at 5:00 AM, the ground in front of me illuminated by my headlamp. With only a small breeze blowing, the loudest noise was the high-pitched squeak of the snow as it crunched underfoot.

I paused on the way to shut off my headlamp and let my eyes adjust to the darkness, hoping to see a silhouette of the mountains around me so I could make sure I was pointed in exactly the right direction. Up ahead, I could tell that Denali Pass was obscured by some clouds. Over to my right—to the south—were also a couple of spots where I couldn't see. It made me hesitate. It was too dark to tell if the clouds over Denali Pass were just lofty or if they were lenticular clouds.

I turned on my headlamp and started walking again, then stopped, consumed with second thoughts. *This doesn't feel right,* I told myself. I turned around and started heading back toward my tent.

I took about ten steps, then stopped once more. *What the fuck are you doing?* I scolded myself. *What are you afraid of?* Sure, the weather was not picture perfect, but it was decent. This was my chance. Was the altitude messing with my thought process? I was all dressed up and ready to go. If the weather turned really bad, I could head back then. Really, it was now or never.

"Oh, what the hell," I said and turned around and marched toward the summit in earnest. I put my mind into full expedition mode.

When I reached the Autobahn—the dangerous slope responsible for more deaths than any other on the mountain—I was relieved to find it in good condition. Another stroke of luck. About a foot of soft snow covered the slope, just enough to provide good footing and not so deep as to make it an impossible struggle. But no matter what the footing, advancing at that altitude requires slow, deliberate motions. I "rest stepped"—a technique mountaineers use to briefly pause with every step, resting all their weight on their straightened back leg for just a second before shifting to the other leg. It preserves energy by putting pressure on bone, not muscle, for that brief rest. It feels like walking like a robot.

Once I hit the saddle of Denali Pass at about 18,000 feet, I was relieved to see it wasn't completely marble ice as I had expected it might be. Instead, it was a combination of ice and granular snow commonly called "neve." I was also relieved to find basically no wind. There was enough light in the sky that I could turn my headlamp off. I was nervous about finding my way through the rocks of the pass, but I made it cleanly on my first try. I stopped for a few minutes to hydrate and eat a bit of chocolate, amazed at how well things were going so far.

Next I slogged to the left of Zebra Rocks, the striped monument-like boulders surrounded by wind-scoured ice, and onto what climbers call the Football Field plateau at 19,000 feet. From there, I had to take a steep slope up to the summit ridge to make my way to the top. By then, I had been in almost constant motion for more than seven hours. I remembered there was a virtual fork in the route at the Football Field.

Everything in my memory told me, *Don't go left. Don't go left.* Going left meant climbing a steeper incline that was more prone to avalanches. I knew it probably wasn't a good route to take. I remembered that I had gone to the right when I climbed the mountain with Buck and Tom, but I couldn't remember exactly how we had done it. Now, four and a half years later and in the dead of winter, there were absolutely no tracks or wands from other climbers to follow. I would have to crawl around what looked like a small icefall, and I wasn't sure how I would do it. If I went the wrong way and had to turn back after several hundred yards, I would kick myself. I wouldn't have the time or the energy to try to go the other way and still summit. I had to make a decision. Going right would be safer, but I might not find the route. Left, I knew, was more dangerous but also more direct.

I decided to go left.

It turned out to be incredibly hard work. The route was filled with knee-deep snow, unusual for that altitude on Denali at that time of year. Ultracold temperatures typically mean less precipitation.

I kicked in a step with my crampons, inhaled two big breaths, then kicked in another step.

Kick.

Breathe. Breathe.

Kick.

Surely I was moving too slowly, I thought, remembering our slow pace in summer 2010. Would I have the energy to make it? I was postholing—one leg sinking deep into snow, then the other—up a steep incline.

Just keep going. One foot in front of the other, I told myself. *I'm sooo close.*

At one point, on a steep section just before the ridge, I stopped for maybe thirty seconds to rest, half sobbing and half grunting from exhaustion. I could feel my lungs ache with effort in the thin air. I was also uncomfortable up there with only one axe, wishing I had brought both for that spot. I had to swing hard overhead through thick snow to find purchase for my pick and punch deep steps with my feet to make sure I was secure. After a half minute of boo-hooing, I pulled my shit back together.

Nearing my 2:00 PM cutoff time, I reached a daunting, nearly vertical twenty-foot section just prior to the ridge that sits directly across from the massive cornice near Denali's summit. I climbed to the top of that section, thrust my axe into the ridge, and pulled myself up onto it. Standing on the ridge, my toes near frostbite from jamming them into the front of my boots while kicking steps, I stopped for a breather before continuing. I looked straight ahead as I walked on the wide north-sloping ridge leading to the summit. After about fifty yards, there it was. I could actually see it.

The summit.

Up until that moment, I wasn't truly sure if I was going to make it. I hadn't trusted Denali, hadn't felt assured that everything would come together just right—the weather, the snow conditions, my body. Finally, it seemed assured.

With numb fingers, I pulled my GoPro camera from my pocket and strapped it across my head. Crunching my way up the ridge, steadying myself with my ice axe handle, I gasped for air with each step, grunting occasionally through the mass of ice hanging from my beard.

Then my good fortune continued: the sky opened clear and deep blue above me. Off to my right the sun hung low, casting a warm glow on the snowy peaks all around me. Denali's often ferocious winds barely whispered. It must have been about minus forty-five degrees, not bad by winter standards.

Up ahead, I spotted a small pole sticking up with a flat disk on it, a manmade object in this natural world: the summit marker.

I plodded toward it. When I got there, I fell to my knees and brushed the snow from the marker with my furry mitten. I couldn't help but weep.

"It's January eleventh. It's two o'clock," I said. "I'm at the top of Denali."

I looked around at the beauty and continued to bawl. I couldn't have felt more grateful to be there. I was so glad to have accomplished my goal. This had been, without question, the most exhausting, risky, and mentally tough expedition I had ever experienced. So much trial and error. So much discomfort. So much soul-searching.

At long last, I reached the summit of Denali at two o'clock in the afternoon on January 11, 2015.

As I stood alone at the top of North America in the bitter cold, my mind raced. I considered what had driven me there. Was it ego, the need to be first? Was it the sheer desire to experience something unique on this earth? Was it learning how I could move forward in the world solo?

When I first started planning to attempt a solo ascent of Denali, I had not fully anticipated that it would take four years of effort. The constantly changing weather and extreme physical work on steep inclines at high altitude had taken me well out of my cold-loving comfort zone.

I knew I couldn't stand there long. I was exhausted and a long way from camp in the thin air. I still faced substantial danger in getting back down.

A million thoughts floated through my head in the ten minutes I spent on the summit. "Oh my," was all I could articulate between deep breaths in that final moment. "Oh my gosh."

Chapter 22

Long Way Home

As I turned to head down for the long journey back to camp, I thought about how magnificent our earth is. Tall, lifeless frozen peaks and glaciers lead to lush, tree-filled valleys that extend all the way to oceans, deserts, and tropical jungles. How did we get so lucky to live in this splendor?

I started down a slightly different way than I came up. The route would be a little longer but less steep and much easier to traverse.

"Going to get the hell out of here," I said into my recorder, my thoughts rambling with exhaustion. "Oh my God, what a day. That was hell. Ugh. . . . Toes are frozen; fingers are pretty good but . . . oh shit. Just hope the weather is gonna hold for me to get down. . . . Oh man, what a view."

Gravity is a friend to a descending climber's lungs as breathing becomes increasingly less labored, but it's an enemy to stability on steep declines. It is much more difficult to see the terrain below you and to find good footing. Thighs start to burn after a while, and knees feel crunched with the weight of each step. The long, steep, open slope downward can be scary, leaving you feeling exposed. It's easy to imagine tumbling down in a forward fall.

After carefully digging in my heels as I lurched down a ridgeline, I made it through the worst of the Autobahn as night fell, my eyes slowly adjusting to the dim twilight reflecting on the snow. Just then, I heard the faint sound of a motor growing louder and louder. After a few minutes, Talkeetna Air Taxi's Turbo Otter came into view, first as a speck against the backdrop of craggy mountains, then plainly soaring overhead. I smiled. That had to be my friend Paul at the controls, coming with a photographer to check on me. They must have received my SPOT signal and known that I had summited.

As the plane made a pattern of long passes over the mountain, it became clear that Paul was still searching for me. I switched on

After receiving my SPOT signal that I had reached the summit, Paul Roderick flew up to search for me and make sure I was okay. A small dot of light from my headlamp was barely visible from the plane over the Autobahn. *Photo by John Walter Whittier*

my headlamp and tried to shine it toward the plane as it made its last pass. I hoped they had seen my tiny light.

As I continued down the mountain, brimming with my own excitement, I couldn't allow myself to get too wrapped up in my thoughts. The mountain was still dangerous. Most fatalities happen on the descent, I reminded myself over and over. I needed to maintain my focus.

The closer I got to the security of my tent waiting for me at 17,200 feet, the more confident I felt. I couldn't help but rejoice inside. *Holy crap!* I thought. *I can't believe I made it!*

I had never really thought about how I would react—how anyone would react—after so many years of trying to complete this singular goal. I try not to think about the finish line when I'm on expeditions. It's better to live in the moment, focused on the tasks at hand. But there I was, the goal finally accomplished.

I started thinking about all the people who had helped me on this long journey, and I was eager to thank them and share my joy. Stevie had been closest to me emotionally along the way. With daily phone calls, she had heard about every accomplishment and every setback, her hopes wrapped up in my journey. I was eager to tell her the details of my last couple of days. I hoped she hadn't worried about me too much. Paul had flown in sometimes-difficult conditions to check on me and ferry me in and out each time. I couldn't wait to shake his hand. And then there were all the climbers back in Talkeetna—a small community I had come to know and love over the years. They knew the mountain and truly understood what I had been facing. By my fourth solo trip, Talkeetna felt like my second home, and I was eager to land back there and celebrate with my friends.

Later, I would call my mom. I would call Jacob. I would call Buck. I knew they would be relieved more than anything, glad I had gotten that stick out of my ass once and for all. I think they had hoped I would just give up, but they also knew I'm like a dog on a bone when it comes to these expeditions.

Thinking about all of them, I assessed what this Denali quest had meant. Scaling that mountain all alone, suffering through so much hardship, and wallowing in moments of bliss had taught me more about who I am.

Was I a loner? No. I like being among friends and socializing. But I did find out that I am capable of more than even I had imagined, and that I'm okay being completely alone for a while.

I learned that I can improvise well on my own.

I learned that I can train my brain to cope with most anything.

I learned not to let small annoyances get under my skin. What seems like an emergency often is not. Even by ourselves, we can get through more than we have ever imagined.

Perhaps more importantly, I learned that experiences are best when shared with others. Friends and family bring balance to life, giving us other perspectives that make us healthier in our pursuit of happiness.

A solo expedition is okay now and again, but journeys are much more fulfilling when you can reflect on them with someone. Nobody could understand quite what it was like to endure those days stuck in the tent at 11,200 feet, wondering if I would wither away before the storm did. I wouldn't be able to fully convey the feeling that came with seeing that spotlight of the shining moon refracted through the ice.

I made it back to the tent in just over three hours. It had taken me nine hours to climb up from there but only about a third of that time to come back down. My tent felt cozy that night as I indulged in a feast. I gathered a bunch of the food that the raven had gotten into but not devoured, a collection of several entrees including some peas, potatoes, and hopefully no bird shit. It was a mess of warm, gooey calories, and it tasted wonderful after such a hard day.

Afterward, I popped an ibuprofen to dull the aches in my muscles and collapsed into my sleeping bag for a good night's sleep. I was exhausted, but I was excited about my accomplishment.

The next day, starting in the early morning darkness, I methodically "down-climbed" several tricky, steep sections. Facing the mountain, I carefully lowered myself down as if on a ladder, an axe in each hand and my feet searching for strong footholds below me. Finally reaching my cave and cache at 14,200 feet, I dug around the bags in search of the working satellite phone. As soon as I found it, I gave Stevie a call.

"Lonnie!" she exclaimed, her melodic voice sounding like sweet music.

"I'm sorry I didn't call," I told her, explaining the snafu with the satellite phones. I asked if she had been worried.

It turned out that she hadn't gotten every beacon signal that I had set off—the one at about 16,000 feet never got through—and she had been worried sick. Forty-eight hours had passed without her hearing from me, and I was twelve hours overdue by the time I reached her. She said she would have sounded the emergency alarm that night if she hadn't heard from me.

She and Paul had seen my SPOT beacon signal on what looked like the summit, but the GPS can be imprecise. When Paul flew up looking for me at dusk, I realized he hadn't spotted me on his first couple of passes. Winds had tossed his small plane around. Gusts near the top of Denali had reached about thirty-five knots, Stevie said, and they were worried I had been caught in a storm. He did locate me later, after I clicked on my headlamp.

Stevie and I talked for about twenty minutes. I told her all about my last couple of days of climbing and asked about the weather forecast for coming down. As I rambled on excitedly, Stevie finally interjected, "So, did you summit?"

I laughed out loud. In all of our conversation, I had never used the word "summit."

"Yes!" I told her. "Yes!"

"Way to go!" she said, then jokingly changed to a businesslike tone. "Got that done."

"Dave Johnston has a sauna and moose stew waiting for you," she added. Johnston was a Talkeetna resident and member of the first team to successfully summit Denali in winter almost a half century earlier. I could now relate to him in a new way. "You'd better hurry up."

I couldn't help but want to go fast on the descent. Each step down brought me more oxygen, more warmth, and more comfort. I always feel a sense of danger on the return from my expeditions. It seems as though there are incidents that take me frighteningly close to disaster, and Denali was no different. On my way to camp at 11,200 feet, I struggled to keep my unruly sled from knocking me down. It either rammed me in the back of my legs or shot past me, threatening to pull me down with it. I stopped on a flat space to make some adjustments to the sled's towlines, and part of the rope got wrapped around my left crampon just as the sled started sliding down the hill. The snagging rope jerked me off my feet. Shit! Would I get pulled off the mountain now in a stupid accident like this?

I slid on my belly, grabbed my ski poles at their bases, and scratched their carbide tips into the ice like a cat's claw. I stopped sliding, but each time I took my hand off my ski pole to untangle the rope from my crampon, I would start sliding again. Finally I managed to get free of the rope and stand upright.

Denali had let me reach the summit, but she still wasn't done messing with me. At 11,200 feet, I got pinned down one more time while snow flurries socked me in. I couldn't believe the irony. Of all the places to get stuck, Denali was going to keep me at the site of my suffer-fest a little longer. I would rather have been stuck any place but there.

Using the time to nurse my blackened toenails and blisters, I thought again about how climate change has affected the world. I had actually felt sleet on Denali during the coldest time of the year.

With clear weather the next morning, I skied straight down the Lower Kahiltna toward base camp, my mouth starting to salivate for the fresh fruit, vegetables, and frothy beer that Stevie was going to deliver there.

I couldn't wait to land in Talkeetna and indulge in a long, hot, soapy shower. I would bathe in three stages: First, I would wash off the chunks. Second, I would lather away the dirt. Third, I would just wallow in the comfort of warm, running water. I could almost feel it streaming down my scalp.

I longed to sit upright on a chair and eat at a table, not hunched over in a tent. I salivated over the thought of the giant standard breakfast at the Roadhouse—a heaping plate of fried potatoes, scrambled eggs, and bacon. A Twister Creek IPA at Denali Brewing across the street would taste heavenly, too.

The flush of a toilet would sound like a symphony.

I reached the base of Heartbreak Hill, the six-hundred-foot incline that descending climbers must ascend to reach base camp—one last, cruel test. My legs were tired, numb, and sweaty as I leaned into the slope. I was in a hurry to rendezvous with the plane. Home was just around the corner.

I hustled to get to the plane's landing strip but watched as Paul's Beaver made a couple of circles and then headed back to Talkeetna.

The winds had picked up, and it was too dangerous to land. Now it was "Heartbreak Base Camp." I tried not to let it bother me. I had stashed several weeks' worth of food and fuel there, so I was safe.

After a night of hard sleep, I noticed the tent walls weren't flapping as much. The tops of nearby Foraker and Hunter were covered with wind-whipped clouds, but as the sun rose, those clouds started to dissipate. I knew then that Paul would be able to land. I laid out black stuff sacks to mark a runway and waited for the familiar *bububububub* sound coming through One Shot Pass.

When the plane approached around midday, the moment felt bittersweet. I was finally going home successful after so many years of trying and coming up short. But this lonely, anguish-filled, and amazing chapter in my life was closing. Soon I would be jolted

Celebrating with Stevie at basecamp. It never felt so good to be going home. *Photo by John Walter Whittier*

back into workaday habits of bills, town life, and the constant hum of motors drowning my thoughts.

I sat atop the supplies on my sled as the plane drew closer and landed into a poof of soft snow. When the propeller came to a stop, I heard the door open and saw two petite legs with big boots dangle, then jump down. Stevie ran as best she could through the deep snow, a giant smile on her face and her big mitten raised in the air to give me a high five.

Epilogue

I hung by my armpits, carefully moving my feet fore and then aft to determine the size of the crevasse I dangled in. Neither of my crampons touched the sides.

Was this how my life would end?

Yes, I was at it again. Two years after soloing Denali in January 2015, I was trying to solo neighboring 14,573-foot Mount Hunter, considered the most difficult "fourteener" in North America. And I was doing it in winter, of course.

Cold and foiled for a second time on the trip by snow that was too deep and soft to traverse, I stopped on the way down and noticed the contour of the snow looked a little different on the flat shelf where I stood. Near a rock wall, I glanced at my little tent far below and took a full step toward it. The snow fell out from under me like a trapdoor under gallows. It was a crevasse, or more precisely a "bergschrund," a deep, dangerous gap where moving glacier meets rock.

Somehow, by instinct or by practicing the move so much that it became a reflex, I managed to drive the shaft of my ice axe into the downhill side of the crack as I fell. With my right arm fully extended and clutched to the head of my axe, my left hand searched for solid snow to grab. When I stopped moving, I tried to compose myself and assess the situation.

If I had any chance of climbing out, I had to first remove the heavy backpack pulling me down and use it as leverage. My body full of adrenaline, I used my left hand to unclip my chest strap and then my waist harness. With my left arm, I reached over my shoulder and grabbed the top pouch of the pack, and with light, short jerks, I pulled the pack overhead and shoved it onto more solid snow above my face. I was now free from its weight but still tethered to it by my right wrist and axe. With my left hand, I unclipped my second axe that was attached to a tool clip on the waist belt of my pack. I managed to run the shaft of the axe through the left shoulder strap securing my pack. I now had the weight of the pack on the downhill side of the lip of the crevasse and two handholds to lever myself out.

Doing a short pull-up on my axes, I swung my left leg up, just managing to get my heel out on the edge of the hole. But I couldn't engage my crampon. I stretched out my right leg as far as I could behind me in the void and snagged the crevasse wall with a couple of teeth on the heel of my crampon. I gave a little push and wiggled like a seal, inching my way up. I got my left leg out farther and gave one more good push with my right, extracting myself from the hole.

After taking a moment to catch my breath, I stood slowly, still in shock, and looked into the hole. It was black and bottomless, and I grew sick to my stomach. That was my first real look at the inside of a crevasse, and it scared the shit out of me. It was time to go home, I told myself. I had been lucky.

A week later, I was back in Minnesota, licking my wounds. But I'll return to Mount Hunter someday. Mountaineering is a part of me now.

My journey to winter climb Denali was one of the hardest of my life. It was my puzzle. Failing to reach the summit three times—and finding the unseen beauty in that failure—helped me solve it.

Once I got back to the comforts of my small cabin in Grand Marais, I quickly forgot the suffering and hardship. The wheels of my brain began to turn, and before spring weather had a chance to melt the snow, I had hatched a plan to scale some mountains in Nepal. That fall, four of us summited the pointy and steep Kyajo Ri, which rises to 20,295 feet. I continue to find and search for significant mountains in North America to climb in winter, both as a team and solo.

Why do I keep climbing? I like the personal challenge of it. I like the extra considerations that come with planning for altitude and figuring out the equations of rope and gear for the technical aspects of ascending steep rock and ice. A mountain is more immediate than the Arctic, too. On a polar expedition, explorers can usually wait out bad weather for as long as it takes, but that isn't an option at high elevation on the side of a mountain. Mountaintops present a more difficult but also more beautiful environment, removed from animals, people, and culture.

I keep honing my technical skills, climbing ice and rock in my spare time to build confidence. I will continue to tackle an occasional solo winter project, too, understanding that it's good to spend time alone every now and then to get lost in my own thoughts.

I am also returning to my old love of exploring the Arctic. I have made it a priority again to undertake projects that contribute to humanity in some way. In 2020, I plan to revisit northern Greenland with a team of explorers and scientists, hoping to cover one thousand miles by dogsled. Calling our expedition "Pulling for the

Planet," we are aiming to examine the effect of climate change on the earth's northernmost community as well as to teach Western society about the Inuit culture's earth-friendly existence and simple values of strong community, family, and ingenuity.

I hope to undertake many other projects after that. I don't keep a bucket list, although at age fifty-seven, I am hearing life's clock ticking louder. I'm fortunate to have made it to this age considering the expeditions I've done. When I was younger, I thought it would be fun to be famous, known for "cool" expeditions. That was a twenty-something mind-set.

There comes a time in your life when, no matter how much you love something, you question the validity of what you're doing. You ask yourself, *Am I making a difference or a contribution in this world?* As I got older and more mature, my journeys became less testosterone-driven and more intellectual. I yearned for experiences with depth and meaning, projects that educated me about our planet, unfamiliar cultures, and myself.

I also realized I could help educate others. While giving presentations, I saw the eyes of fourth-graders widen when I regaled them about my encounters with polar bears. I could see understanding in adults when I presented them with photos and stories as evidence of the warming Arctic and climate change. I love being a conduit of information from my firsthand experiences.

As time marches on, I'm finding it even more difficult to keep my feet planted. I am often reminded that on the grand scale of things, we are on this planet for what amounts to only a nanosecond. I don't want to waste what little time I have. I will continue to explore, to find meaning in each project, as long as my mind and body will allow it.

I can only hope that my expeditions inspire others to take care of our beautiful planet and find happiness through nature. Or at the very least, I hope they inspire people to spend less time on the couch and more time outside. Living in nature elicits a primal existence: eating, sleeping, moving forward, and taking care of our health and our teammates. It is a good reminder for a society that lives in abundance.

In 2016, I started a forum on my website called "Live Simply to Live" as a place to share ideas on how we can find fulfillment through simplicity. By improvising, innovating, and being resourceful—choosing quality over quantity in possessions and experiences—we can consume less and focus on the things that matter most.

I try to lead by example. I live in a 450-square-foot house and will be downsizing to a 250-square-foot cabin that I'm building near a lake in the woods. I grow vegetables, do some canning, and keep a few chickens for eggs. I drive a pieced-together 2008 Toyota Yaris with a homemade lumber rack. I run short errands on my bicycle whenever I can.

I make sure that I do something for the earth by supporting tree-planting projects and leaving as much green space as possible around my small construction projects.

I view our delicate atmosphere like a blue blanket a mother would wrap around her child, protecting us, keeping us safe. This precious gift deserves to be treated with love and respect. Our blanket is getting tattered and thin.

I feel humbled and grateful to be on this wondrous planet, and I remain optimistic and inspired by it.

On one of the last days of my solo canoe trip in the Quetico back in 2009, I saw something that has stayed with me. On a small rock island, a single dwarfed white pine grew out of a crack in the granite. Though its growth had been stunted, it was a perfect specimen, looking like a three-foot bonsai tree.

I stared at it for a while. It's amazing to see something so beautiful growing out of an eight-inch split in solid rock. It gave me hope for the planet, hope that we as humans can live in harmony with nature and persevere, just like that little pine.

Acknowledgments

Where do I begin? So many years, so many wonderful folks who have entered my life and helped in so many ways.

I'm very appreciative to have had Stevie Anna Plummer help me organize all my winter expeditions on Denali. She brought a personal and professional touch to our social media outreach and as liaison with our sponsors. Her journals and her recall of events played a key part in this book. And I am forever grateful for the fresh fruit and salad she always remembered to bring on the plane when picking me up from the mountain.

I want to thank Paul Roderick, Danial Doty, Richard Olmsted, and the wonderful staff at Talkeetna Air Taxi (TAT) for their friendship and outstanding service over the years.

Thanks to John Walter Whittier, who captured the soul of the adventure through his amazing photographs and video, and to Dmitri von Klein for his help in managing the 2013 expedition from Talkeetna and taking images and video that would later be used in our film, *Cold Love*.

Sincere gratitude for the friends I made in Talkeetna, who accommodated my needs and made it feel like a second home: Trisha

Costello and the Talkeetna Roadhouse staff, Denali Brewing, KTNA Radio, Lauri Jo Ricci-stec, Willi and Ellie Prittie, Dave Johnston, and Cari Sayre. I especially want to thank Vern Tejas, who always made time to answer my endless questions about climbing Denali in the winter.

For all the support from my friends at Hear in America: Bob Marshall, Greta Ratliff, Murphy Brock, Richard Williams, and Quinn Pearl.

To the folks at the National Park Service's Talkeetna Ranger Station—Maureen Gualtieri, Joe Reichert, Mark Westman, Tucker Chenoweth, and Missy Smothers: thank you for the wealth of help and information.

On the home front, I'd like to thank Mark Hansen for helping me design and build my birch skis; my good friends Buck Benson and Tom Surprenant for supporting my projects over the years and for the great memories we shared on Denali; and Jeff and Sue Gecas of the Gunflint Tavern, my first stop for food and drink whenever I return home.

I'm grateful to have met Pascale Marceau, who loves climbing as much as I do. I appreciate her second set of eyes throughout the writing of this book and her help with creating several of the appendices. Around the time this book is released, we will be coming off climbs in Canada's Yukon and British Columbia.

My first introduction to Pam Louwagie was when I got a call from her at my home in Grand Marais just after my return from Denali in 2015. She wanted to interview me about the climb for the *Star Tribune*. I didn't know what I would say that had not already been said, but I soon realized that her questions, though sometimes hard to answer, were different from the rest. With remarkable attention to detail, she was good at digging into the nitty-gritty and, in the end, produced for the newspaper an accurate account of what I had experienced. My emotions welled up as I relived it all. It was a kind of therapy, allowing me to realize that everything is okay now. I knew then that if I were to write a book about my experience, I would want Pam to coauthor it with me. Thank you, Pam, for working with an unconventional, old-fashioned, and occasionally grumpy co-writer for the last year and a half.

Thank you Minnesota Historical Society Press and Josh Leventhal for believing in our book from that very first meeting.

Finally, special thanks go to my longtime sponsors PrimaLoft and Granite Gear, who year after year continue to support and believe in my crazy ideas.

—Lonnie Dupre

~

I first met Lonnie Dupre in January 2015, when I interviewed him for a *Star Tribune* story right after his successful solo summit of Denali. His humility and enthusiasm were evident from the get-go, and I am thankful for his patience and good humor during my endless questions about climbing and outdoor survival as we wrote this book. Thank you, Lonnie, for entrusting me to help tell your story of perseverance. It was an honor to learn from your optimistic spirit.

Thanks also to all the people who helped in the research and editing of this book. We are grateful to the editors at the Minnesota Historical Society Press, especially to Josh Leventhal for his guidance and understanding while working with coauthors who live 250 miles apart, and to Shannon Pennefeather for her careful eyes and seeing this book through to production. Thanks to Maureen Gualtieri and other staff members at Denali National Park, who were quick to respond to all sorts of inquiries, including questions about the history of the mountain and the people who have climbed it. Thanks to editors at the *Star Tribune* for the initial assignment to write about Lonnie's feat for the newspaper, and for allowing me time away from work to take on this book-writing project.

Hearty thanks to author and editor Laurie Hertzel for years of always managing to give me just the right advice on writing narrative nonfiction; to author Ron Handberg for his book-writing insight and feedback; to Kate Parry for her guidance and support; to Joe Williams for the book-writing pep talks; to my attorney brother, Vince Louwagie, for looking out for me legally and to my sister and brother-in-law, Jolene Louwagie and Kevin Knutson, for their eagle eyes on the text.

Thanks to family and friends for putting up with my long absences during this project. Thanks most of all to my husband, Mitch Rauk, for his storytelling know-how and his steadfast encouragement and patience.

—Pam Louwagie

APPENDICES

Divvying Up Weights

A Method for Fair Distribution of Expedition Supplies across a Team

Pascale Marceau and Lonnie Dupre

Over the years, on various types of expeditions (polar travel and mountaineering), we have noticed that divvying up gear among expedition team members is both an art and a science. Our method for figuring out how much weight each teammate should pull or carry is derived simply from experience. There is no laboratory or sport-kinetic research to what we present below.

Although there is an endless number of variables when it comes to the human body, we narrow our approach based on three factors:

1. Body weight
2. Gender
3. Age

One key assumption is that each team member has an equal base fitness level for the expedition and no limiting injuries. Observe caution with this assumption. It is often the case that fitness is significantly different among individuals: these rules of thumb should be used to determine a baseline that can then be adjusted to account for fitness disparities and limitations. Also note that at times, objects that are awkward or difficult to haul or carry may break these generic rules of thumb.

SANITY CHECK

Before you start, check the total weight the team will have to carry. Our goal is to ensure backpack weights remain below one-third of a person's body weight. This is different for hauling a sled, of course. If it looks as if the team is faced with exceedingly large loads, consider bringing a sled if the route allows or know that relaying loads may be required in the early days of the expedition.

When altitude and acclimatization come into play, maximum backpack weights should be about one-quarter of body weight. Once again, more can be accommodated with sleds. According to veteran mountaineer Willi Prittie, "a very fit person can shoot themselves in the foot very rapidly at high altitudes by pushing just a little too hard too early on a high-altitude expedition and both slow their acclimatization rate and make themselves about two or three times more likely to develop HAPE [high-altitude pulmonary edema] or HACE [high-altitude cerebral edema] or both. This is especially true with climbers inexperienced at altitude."

BODY WEIGHT

Gear is divided proportionally to each individual's body weight. There is a reason wrestling and martial arts have weight categories. It's no different on the mountain or the ice floes. That being said, the bigger you are, the more absolute weight you can carry, but there is a diminishing return on percentage, meaning the smaller you are, the higher percentage of your body weight you can handle. So rather than doing some complicated math to determine the log relation, let's just say if there's a bit extra to carry, give it to the smallest person—counterintuitive but fair.

GENDER

Female teammates get to shed a bit of weight; eight percent is our multiplier. That weight gets picked up by their male counterparts. There's no denying there are some super-strong women out there who could outperform their male counterparts by carrying monster loads, but these ratios are based on an average representation of the genders.

AGE

Let's face it. The older you get, the more your muscular strength declines and your muscle recovery times increase. It's only fair to shed some of that load to the younger teammates. Again, some maintain incredible fitness into their seventies, but those folks had to work extra hard to be there. We're considering average fitness for all here. We use an age multiplier of 0.5 percent gear weight for every year above or below the team's median age. So if your team spans a huge range, then yes, the youngest folks will carry significantly more than the older members. Such is life!

The reality is that the team will not know exact weights and will not be carrying a spreadsheet to do this, so often these ratios are simply estimated, just as everyone's allocated gear pile weight will be estimated. It's still good to have these adjusting ratios in mind and to have discussed them with the team prior to that fun moment when the gear is yard-saled in the snow and it's time to load up the packs and/or sleds.

Following is an example of one of our team mountaineering expeditions to climb Mount Hunter in Alaska.

Team Composition

Teammate	Body Weight (pounds)	Gender	Age
Willi	190	M	62
Lonnie	152	M	55
Pascale	135	F	40
Chris	200	M	30

Total expedition team gear, after we dropped our sleds, to be carried in backpacks: 180 pounds.

Step 1: Sanity Check

Teammate	Body Weight (pounds)	⅓ Body Weight (pounds)
Willi	190	63
Lonnie	152	51
Pascale	135	45
Chris	200	67
		226

The total weight of 226 pounds, one-third of our body weights, is below the 180 pounds we need to carry = good!

Step 2: Body Weight Multiplier

Teammate	Body Weight (pounds)	Weight Multiplier	Equal Distribution (pounds)	Body Weight Adjusted Distribution (pounds)
Willi	190	28%	45	50
Lonnie	152	22%	45	40
Pascale	135	20%	45	36
Chris	200	30%	45	53

Step 3: Gender Factor

Teammate	Gender	Gender Factor	Body Weight and Gender Adjusted Distribution (pounds)
Willi	M	+8% / 3	51.5
Lonnie	M	+8% / 3	41
Pascale	F	–8%	33
Chris	M	+8% / 3	54

Step 4: Age Multiplier

Teammate	Age	Years Above Team's Median Age Span	Age Multiplier .5% for every year above median	Body Weight and Gender and Age Adjusted Distribution (pounds)
Willi	62	16	–8%	47
Lonnie	55	9	–4.5%	40
Pascale	40	–6	3%	34
Chris	30	–16	8%	58

Step 5: Final Results and Sanity Check

Teammate	Body Weight (pounds)	Gender	Age	Adjusted Weight Distribution (pounds)	⅓ Body Weight (pounds)
Willi	190	M	62	**47**	63
Lonnie	152	M	55	**40**	51
Pascale	135	F	40	**34**	45
Chris	200	M	30	**58**	67

Poor Chris carries a heavy load, but let's be clear: he's still well under his one-third body weight, and he is a tall, fit, strapping, young man. Willi seems heavy, but he too is tall and heavy. Lucky Pascale seems to get a free ride. The reality is, she's significantly lighter than the rest of the team.

How to Keep Feet Warm at −60°F

The key to keeping your feet warm in extreme cold temperatures starts with good boots. Inevitably, the question of what constitutes a good boot has some trade-offs. The more supportive and stiffer the boot, the colder your feet are going to be regardless of insulation. That is why even in the best mountaineering boots, people sometimes lose toes. The boot may have plenty of insulation, but the rigidity of the boot restricts circulation. At the same time, for mountaineering, rigid support is essential to hold crampons, for front pointing, and for those steep and rugged pitches and ridges.

On the other end of the spectrum are soft-bottom mukluks or kamiks used by the Inuit or Athabascan people. The warmest of these designs are made from smoke- and brain-tanned moose hide. They feel like bedroom slippers, offering lots of room for circulation and for wiggling chilly toes. They are also extremely light, putting no added stress on legs during those long ski or snowshoe runs. The downside is that they offer little to no support, making it difficult to get good footing and resulting in sore feet at the end of the day.

Depending on your planned activity, it is up to you to determine how much or how little support and insulation you will need in your footwear. Whether it is a stiff boot or a soft one, I layer my feet as follows:

Foot, from skin outward: thin wool liner sock; a vapor barrier liner (heavy-duty plastic bag; I use maple sap bags); a medium-weight wool/synthetic PrimaLoft blend sock; then a heavyweight hand-knitted, loose wool outer sock. The vapor barrier sock is key to keep your outer socks and boot liners dry.

Boot, moving from sock outward: an insulated synthetic felt boot liner with reflective aluminum; then an insulated insole of synthetic felt with perforated reflective Mylar; beneath it add a PrimaLoft Aerogel insole, and at the bottom a perforated mesh/waffle insole to capture snow and frost. Thicknesses of insoles and liners will depend on temperature needs.

For mountaineering boots, I make sure the boot has a good lace system with beefy laces that will not cut your fingers. I minimize the use of Velcro. In extreme cold, one way to mitigate cold feet in rigid technical boots is to loosen the laces when not on technical terrain and cinch them only on technical segments. I also select a boot that is one or two sizes too big. This way you can add an extra insulted insole and extra thick wool socks, always allowing plenty of space to wiggle toes.

In extreme cold, I use Forty Below Purple Haze overboots as an extra layer on my feet.

Clothing, Equipment, and Food List

Here is a detailed list of the clothing, equipment, and food systems that I recommend for exploration in extreme climates. It is the culmination of all I have learned from my polar and Arctic trips along with my Denali winter climbs. I believe these supplies offer the perfect balance of lightweight yet reliable systems to keep one alive in prolonged extreme cold.

One's gear and food list is a perpetual work in progress. I enjoy tweaking my systems and testing out new gear in hopes of always improving what I carry up the mountain or onto the ice.

CLOTHING

Bodywear

1 pair Merino wool boxer briefs—wool okay here because body
    heat keeps them warm even if moist
Brynje of Norway fishnet top and bottom polyester long underwear
Patagonia Capilene Thermal Weight 92% polyester long underwear
    with open grid pattern
PrimaLoft insulated zipper pants—left behind at 14,000-foot camp,
    where I switched to the one-piece down suit

Wintergreen 3-ply Supplex nylon breathable bib pants
Long-sleeve midweight zip-neck top with a zippered chest
    pocket
PrimaLoft lightweight vest
PrimaLoft down blend lightweight parka with hood
Wintergreen 3-ply Supplex nylon breathable wind shell anorak
PrimaLoft down blend high-fill vest or PrimaLoft belay parka
One-piece down suit

Hands

Fleece liner gloves
Windstopper outer gloves
Custom-knitted wool mitts with lanolin—lanolin keeps moisture
    out of fibers, easier to dry
Smoke-tanned leather wolverine overmitts
Breathable wind shell overmitts—not Gore-Tex; breathable Supplex
    fabric

Head and Face

Wolverine ruff on wind-shell hood—best for shedding frost, great
    wind protection
Seirus neoprene face mask
Lightweight fleece neck gaiter
Goggles with flat/low-light lens

Footwear

Merino wool thin liner sock
Vapor barrier sock—I use a heavy-duty plastic bag used for
    collecting maple syrup for complete barrier protection
Fox River PrimaLoft wool blend medium-weight sock

Heavyweight wool socks—mine are from the Faroe Islands, hand-
knitted wool with lanolin; lanolin keeps moisture out of fibers,
easier to dry
Boreal G1 Lite mountaineering boots
Synthetic felt liner or Finnish wool tossu
Insoles—waffle bottom to catch frost
Forty Below Purple Haze overboots
Forty Below synthetic camp booties

EQUIPMENT

2 MSR WhisperLite International cookstoves plus 1 stove repair kit
and 1 extra (third) pump
11 (22-ounce) fuel bottles—provides fuel for 33 days (7 ounces
fuel/day)
Homemade ¼-inch plywood stove board with stove and fuel bottle
holder
4 lighters—I wear one on a string around my neck
Homemade reflective pocket oven made of foil bubble
wrap—for boil-in-a-bag meals to retain the heat to allow
cooking
Hilleberg Unna or Soulo tent
Homemade foam tent floor—band-fold design made of
Isotherm
2 snow stakes
26-ounce Thermos
Titanium single-wall mug with handle
Anodized aluminum bowl
Spoon
Snow saw—full-size carpenter's handsaw with ripsaw teeth; cuts
through snow easily, has push–pull handle, ripsaw teeth

are a little bigger; cuts good snow blocks for building snow
caves or tent shelter walls.

Voile shovel with extendable D-handle

2 technical mountaineering axes with bent shaft: Black Diamond
Venom hammer and adze—hockey-tape the head and
upper grip for daggering and plunging

Spinner leash—if desired but could go no leashes

Black Diamond Sabretooth 14-point mountaineering crampons

5 carabiners—wide gate, easy to operate with mitts on; 2 to pull
sled, 1 on sled bridle to avoid rope burn, 1 for ascender,
1 spare

Glacier harness for ascending and rappelling the fixed lines or
Swiss seat made of webbing

Anchor tie-in safety leash

Petzl Basic ascender—also used for rappelling

2 Prusik cords—for rappel backup, ascending, holding the crevasse
pole, etc.

Petzl Spatha knife

Plastic 6-foot expedition sled

14-foot crevasse pole (recommend: 2×80–inch sections of 1¼-inch
aluminum pipe held together by dowel and cotter pin; in
2015, I used a spruce pole)

PrimaLoft synthetic –15°F sleeping bag

Montbell Spiral down –25°F sleeping bag

Western Mountaineering HotSac VBL vapor barrier liner bag made
with reflective Mylar

Primus cook pot—2 liter; nice to melt snow in larger quantities

Birch skis—homemade, wide and long to maximize the dispersing
weight to improve flotation; ski as long as airline will allow

(80–115 inches) to better span crevasses; ski built for
width of a mountaineering boot binding (4–5 inches) to
prevent drag

Skins—glued and screwed onto skis

2 Black Diamond carbon fiber poles—collapsible with cork handles
to keep hands warm

Therm-a-Rest Z Lite Sol, cut to ¾ length—I use this as first layer
under my bag to keep moisture off the bag

Therm-a-Rest NeoAir XTherm inflatable air mattress—I use this
under the Z Lite foam pad

Granite Gear Rolwaling backpack 75–80 liters

Sled bag, large, elongated duffel—no need to be
waterproof

1-liter Nalgene water bottle with Granite Gear insulated sleeve

3 large compression sacks—for sleeping bag, insulated clothing,
miscellaneous clothing

175 (4-foot) bamboo wands with black and reflective duct tape

2 Voile straps to fasten gear to pack

Outdoor thermometer

Deuter 3-liter hydration pack with insulated sleeve and tube for
summit day

Granite Gear silicone nylon summit pack

Electronics

Some of this equipment remains at 14,000 feet with the sled:

2 satellite phones—one Iridium and one Globalstar

Cell phone—for sending out images; there is cell reception
(if lucky) in three locations

2 GoPro cameras

Custom monopod with camera attachment—I do not use my
  trekking pole because you may not pick it up until on the way
  back down
Digital point-and-shoot camera—Canon PowerShot G15
Transistor radio—for news, weather, and sanity
Petzl headlamp—internal battery
Black Diamond headlamp—external battery
40 AA lithium batteries
20 AAA lithium batteries
2 (12-volt) custom cold-weather AA battery charger with female
  12-volt socket
Male 12v-to-USB adapter
USB cable
SPOT Gen3 satellite personal tracker
Soft padded storage case for electronics
iPod with 2 pairs earbuds because earbuds break easily

Personal

Moist towelettes
Watch with alarm clock—I wear this around my neck on a
  string
Nalgene pee bottle
Toothbrush, toothpaste, floss
Diary—small Rite in the Rain notebook
2 pens—which need warming to work

Medical Kit

Please consult with your doctor regarding all medications.
Ibuprofen—for inflammation
Aspirin—for joint pain

Excedrin Migraine—a blend of aspirin, acetaminophen, and
   caffeine; excellent for altitude headaches
Oxycodone—a prescription opioid used to treat moderate to
   severe pain
Ambien (zolpidem)—a sedative used for the treatment of
   insomnia, safe at altitude since it does not affect breathing
Flagyl (metronidazole)—an antibiotic that treats giardiasis and
   bacterial infections of the vagina, stomach, skin, joints, and
   respiratory tract; also useful for a burst appendix
Z-Pak (azithromycin)—a common antibiotic used to treat
   pneumonia and bronchitis among other infections; this is
   used only in case you catch an infection before you leave
High-altitude drugs:
   Nifedipine—treatment of high-altitude pulmonary edema
   (HAPE) by reducing pulmonary arterial pressure
   Dexamethasone—a cortisol used in the treatment of high-
   altitude cerebral edema (HACE) as well as high-altitude
   pulmonary edema (HAPE) by suppressing inflammation
   Diamox (acetazolamide)—used to prevent and reduce the
   symptoms of altitude sickness
Antifungal cream
Dermatone—face, lips, fingers, feet; prevents frostbite
Moleskin
Athletic tape
Oximeter—optional, information only

Repair Kit

Wire
Multitool
Sewing kit—needle, thread, collapsible scissors

Zip ties

¾-inch Fastec buckle

Duct tape

Fabric repair tape for tent repair

Aluminum sleeve for tent pole and ski pole repair

Extra tent pole section

Reading glasses for magnifying during repairs in the dark—stove,
    sewing

10 feet of parachute cord

FOOD

Food is an art. This is true in the mountains, too. Over the years, I
have learned what works for me. Meals are a careful balance of the
following attributes: cooking ease, lightweight, hearty, easy to digest,
and savory. I keep most of my fat separate from my meals in the
form of oil, adding it as needed depending on cold and workload.

For a Denali solo winter climb, I bring enough food for 33 days.

Breakfast

Huevos rancheros homemade with dehydrated salsa, powdered
    eggs, refried beans, potatoes, and hummus

Homemade granola with powdered goat milk

Rice pudding

Lunch

Bacon—precooked

Homemade beef jerky—Bragg Liquid Aminos soy sauce and maple
    syrup

Dried Finnish sourdough/rye bread

Nuts—pecans, macadamia nuts, Brazil nuts

Pumpkin seeds

Homemade energy bars, wrapped in waxed paper—nut butters, unsweetened coconut, diced apricots or cranberries, honey, oats, clarified butter

Homemade polar truffles—chocolate, cream, coconut, macadamia nuts, orange liqueur

Ritter Sport chocolate bars—my favorites: Rum Raisins Hazelnuts and Coconut

Honey Stinger Energy Chews—for summit day

PROBAR energy bar—my favorite: Koka Moka

Dinner

Duck fat and/or grapeseed oil and/or olive oil—added to all suppers

Lentil pea soup—dehydrated lentil and split pea soup mixes combined

Mashed potatoes—dehydrated peas and/or corn, powdered potatoes, and bacon

Soba noodle (buckwheat noodle) with Parmesan and tomato base

Couscous with Parmesan and spices

Mac and cheese using egg noodles

Mountain House Pro-Pak dinners—chili mac and lasagna are my favorites

Spices—garlic salt, cayenne

Beverages

Tea—lemon ginger; helps digest fat, good on the stomach

Coffee—Starbucks VIA Instant singles

Russian tea—homemade blend of Tang lemonade, iced tea, cloves, cinnamon, etc.

Hot chocolate made with goat milk

Live Simply to Live

Following are principles and ideas I try to live by to enrich my life and help minimize climate change. How can you do what makes you happy? Try these strategies:

SIMPLIFY

Quality over quantity: that goes both for material possessions and for experiences.

Little stuff = little problems. Big stuff = big problems (mortgage, credit debt, etc.).

Focus on living simply so you can have more time and energy for the things that matter to you.

Be resourceful, improvise, innovate, be self-sufficient.

Buy stuff that lasts and is multipurpose.

RUN YOUR OWN LIFE

Live with purpose.

Shift to a healthy lifestyle; it's good for mind and planet.

Exemplifying a happy, healthy lifestyle is contagious.

Spend more time outdoors; be active.

Surround yourself with like-minded folks.

Making money takes energy; put that energy into learning to live with less.

Be proactive; invest in renewable energies, and vote for politicians who care about the environment, education, and health.

Enjoy the fruits of your labor, provide to those less fortunate, do what feels right in your heart, and enjoy pursuing your dreams.

About the Authors

During a career spanning twenty-five years, LONNIE DUPRE has traveled more than fifteen thousand miles throughout the high Arctic and polar regions by dog team, ski, and kayak. He has lived and traveled with the Polar Inuit, learning from these hardy people and developing a deep appreciation for their culture and way of life. He believes deeply in one's ability to overcome the

© One World Endeavors

seemingly insurmountable obstacles that may stand between an individual and his or her dream.

Dupre's significant achievements include the first west-to-east, three-thousand-mile winter crossing of Canada's famed Northwest Passage by dog team; the first solo January ascent of Denali, North America's highest peak; the world's first circumnavigation of Greenland; and a summer expedition to the North Pole. During his travels over the Arctic's disappearing ice, Dupre has participated in both scientific research and cultural exchanges, working with and gathering data for organizations such as the National Geographic Society, Greenpeace, the Explorers Club, the National Snow and Ice Data Center, and the US Department of Atmospheric Sciences.

Dupre has received worldwide attention for his explorations, including from such media outlets as *Australian Geographic*, CBS *Early Show*, CNN, Discovery Channel, EOS/*Scientific American*, *International Herald Tribune*, *Mother Jones*, MPR, National Geographic (television and magazine), NPR, *New York Times*, *Sports Illustrated*, the *Tonight Show*, *USA Today*, the *Wall Street Journal*, and *Wired Magazine*. Dupre is a Rolex Award for Enterprise Laureate and Fellow National of the Explorers Club. Dupre's Denali climb was named to *Outside* magazine's list of Most Badass Adventures of 2015.

He has authored two previous books: *Greenland Expedition: Where Ice Is Born* and *Life on Ice: 25 Years of Arctic Exploration*.

Lonnie was born and raised on a Minnesota farm. He is descended on his mother's side from Jacques Cartier, the French explorer and founder of Quebec. Lonnie lives in Grand Marais, Minnesota.

Pam Louwagie is an award-winning reporter at the *Star Tribune* in Minneapolis, where she writes everything from breaking news stories to in-depth features about notable people throughout Minnesota. She is the author of the e-book *Saving Bobbi: One Girl's Descent into the World of Child Sex Trafficking*, published by the newspaper. Louwagie first wrote about Lonnie Dupre's successful winter solo summit of

© Glen Stubbe

Denali for the *Star Tribune* shortly after he descended the mountain in 2015. Before joining the *Star Tribune*, she wrote for the *Philadelphia Inquirer* and the *Times-Picayune* in New Orleans. In her spare time, Louwagie loves to run, hike, and camp in the woods of northern Minnesota as well as backpack in national parks and trek in wilderness abroad. She lives in Minneapolis with her husband.